ORELA®

Social Science Practice Questions

Mometrix
TEST PREPARATION

Dear Future Exam Success Story

First of all, **THANK YOU** for purchasing Mometrix study materials!

Second, congratulations! You are one of the few determined test-takers who are committed to doing whatever it takes to excel on your exam. **You have come to the right place.** We developed these practice tests with one goal in mind: to deliver you the best possible approximation of the questions you will see on test day.

Standardized testing is one of the biggest obstacles on your road to success, which only increases the importance of doing well in the high-pressure, high-stakes environment of test day. Your results on this test could have a significant impact on your future, and these practice tests will give you the repetitions you need to build your familiarity and confidence with the test content and format to help you achieve your full potential on test day.

Your success is our success

We would love to hear from you! If you would like to share the story of your exam success or if you have any questions or comments in regard to our products, please contact us at **800-673-8175** or **support@mometrix.com**.

Thanks again for your business and we wish you continued success!

Sincerely,
The Mometrix Test Preparation Team

Printed in the United States of America

Table of Contents

Practice Test #1

1. Which of these pre-Columbian civilizations was Mesoamerican rather than Andean?

a. Inca
b. Aztec
c. Moche
d. Cañaris

2. Which of the following is NOT a correct statement regarding the Pilgrims?

a. The Pilgrims left England in 1620 on the ship known as the *Mayflower* and landed at Cape Cod.
b. The Pilgrims were led by William Bradford with a charter from the London Company.
c. The Pilgrims were a group of Puritans who left England to escape religious persecution.
d. The Pilgrims were a group of separatists who migrated to leave the Church of England.

3. Which of the following is NOT true regarding the early colonization of New York?

a. Dutch fur traders first created the New Amsterdam settlement on Manhattan Island in 1624.
b. King Charles II of England entitled his brother James to conquer New Amsterdam in 1664.
c. James, Duke of York, prohibited assemblies in New York as he was against representation.
d. Colonel Richard Nicols granted very few civil or political rights to the New York colonials.

4. Which of the following did NOT contribute to differences in the lives of New England colonists vs. the lives of Chesapeake colonists during the 17th century?

a. In Virginia and Maryland, female settlers greatly outnumbered male settlers.
b. New England colonists had significantly longer life expectancies than did Chesapeake colonists.
c. New England colonists had a better organized, more stable society than did Chesapeake colonists.
d. New England colonists had educational advantages over Chesapeake colonists.

5. Which of the following statements is true regarding New Spain in the 1500s?

a. New Spain had not yet developed any kind of class system.
b. The Spanish originally imported Africans to use as slaves for labor.
c. The *hacienda* system eventually gave way to the *encomienda* system.
d. Conquistadores experienced shortages of labor in the New World.

6. Which of the following British generals came to Boston in May of 1775 to push General Thomas Gage to become more aggressive toward the American colonists?

a. William Howe
b. Henry Clinton
c. John Burgoyne
d. All of the above

7. When Americans captured Fort Ticonderoga on Lake Champlain, who led them?

a. Ethan Allen
b. Benedict Arnold
c. Richard Montgomery
d. Ethan Allen and Benedict Arnold

8. Which of the following events happened earliest on the eve of the American Revolution?

a. The Declaration of Independence, drafted mainly by Thomas Jefferson, was officially taken up by America's Second Continental Congress.
b. Thomas Paine published his famous pamphlet, *Common Sense*, influencing even more moderate Americans to agree upon independence.
c. The Second Continental Congress issued the "Olive Branch Petition," begging King George III to ask Parliament to make peace with them.
d. King George III of England approved the Prohibitory Act, an official declaration that the colonists were in rebellion and no longer protected.

9. Which of the following is NOT true with respect to the Constitutional Convention of 1787?

a. The delegates to the Convention had a common opinion that people are inherently selfish.
b. Convention delegate Benjamin Franklin was quite instrumental in the Great Compromise.
c. Edmund Randolph designed the "Virginia Plan," which was introduced by James Madison.
d. Paterson's New Jersey Plan favoring smaller states was an alternative to the Virginia Plan.

10. Which of these was NOT a factor that contributed to the duel in which Aaron Burr killed Alexander Hamilton?

a. Some Federalists who opposed US Western expansion were attempting to organize a movement to secede from the Union.
b. Alexander Hamilton challenged Aaron Burr to a duel because he objected to US expansion into the West, which Burr supported.
c. Secessionist Federalists tried to enlist Aaron Burr's support for their cause by backing him in his run for Governor of New York.
d. Alexander Hamilton was the leader of the group that opposed Aaron Burr's campaign to run for New York Governor.

11. Which of the following was the first canal built in New York State?

a. The Cayuga-Seneca Canal
b. The Chambly Canal
c. The Oswego Canal
d. The Erie Canal

12. Which of the following written works did Thomas Paine publish after the American Revolution?

a. *Common Sense*
b. *Rights of Man*
c. *The Age of Reason*
d. *Rights of Man* and *The Age of Reason*

13. Which of the following is NOT true about the Second Great Awakening?

a. This movement was a reaction against the Enlightenment emphasis on rationalism.
b. This movement emphasized individualized, personalized, emotional religious faith.
c. This movement was characterized by the participation of large numbers of women.
d. This movement's individualistic nature contradicted nationalism and expansionism.

14. Which of the following statements is true regarding movements toward reform in America during the 1840s?

a. American society was undergoing changes, which made conditions unstable and uncertain.
b. During this period of time, the traditional values of American society were being challenged.
c. The Romantic Movement, a reaction to the Enlightenment, was supportive of reforms.
d. All of the above statements are true.

15. Which of the following was an example of violence in cities that occurred as a result of rapid urbanization in America in the 1830s?

a. Democrats opposed Whigs in New York City so strenuously that the state militia was called in.
b. Both New York City and Philadelphia experienced a series of racial riots during the mid-1830s.
c. A Catholic convent was attacked and plundered by a violent mob in New York City in 1834.
d. All of the above occurred in American cities during the 1830s.

16. When was the first American transcontinental railroad finished?

a. 1862
b. 1890
c. 1869
d. 1865

17. Which of the following helped prepare the US for entry into World War I?

a. The National Defense Act
b. The Navy Act
c. The Revenue Act
d. All of the above

18. Of the following demonstrations of Soviet disagreements with the US after World War II, which was the first to transpire?

a. The Soviet Union backed Communist control of Hungary and Romania.
b. The Soviet Union endorsed Communist control of Czechoslovakia.
c. The Soviets did not allow conservatives to serve in the Communist government imposed on Poland.
d. Soviets refused to take part in the international Baruch Plan because they mistrusted American motives.

19. Which of the following most accurately describes the group that invaded the Bay of Pigs in 1961?

a. Members of the US CIA
b. A group of Cuban exiles
c. The people of Cuba
d. CIA-sponsored Cuban exiles

20. Which answer does NOT correctly describe an event leading to the dissolution of the Soviet Union and the end of the Cold War?

a. Older generation Communists successfully staged a coup against Mikhail Gorbachev.
b. Soviet leader Gorbachev initiated Perestroika to restructure the Soviet economy.
c. Soviet leader Gorbachev instituted Glasnost to publicize the Soviet government.
d. The Berlin Wall came down, leading to reunification of East and West Germany.

21. During the Civil Rights era of the 1950s, which of the following events furthered the civil rights cause?

a. The Supreme Court's decision in *Brown v. Board of Education of Topeka*
b. Governor Orval Faubus' actions relative to Little Rock High School
c. Eisenhower's use of the 101st Airborne Division to protect students
d. Both A and C

22. In LBJ's Great Society program, which of the following was NOT included?

a. Medicare
b. Voting rights
c. Federal aid to education
d. Ending the Vietnam War

23. Which of the following statements is NOT true regarding the events of September 11, 2001, in the US?

a. Shortly after that date the US defeated the Taliban and captured Al-Qaeda leader Osama bin Laden.
b. On September 11, 2001, Muslim terrorists flew two hijacked airplanes into the World Trade Center in New York.
c. On September 11, 2001, Muslim terrorists flew a hijacked passenger airliner into the Pentagon in Arlington, Virginia.
d. An airplane hijacked by Muslim terrorists crashed in Pennsylvania after passengers resisted the terrorists.

24. The General Assembly of the Presbyterian Church in 1910 arrived at the "five fundamentals" of Fundamentalism. One of these fundamentals asserted that the Bible was inspired by the Holy Spirit and was therefore true and/or infallible. Which of the following was NOT one of the other four "fundamentals"?

a. Christ was born to a virgin (Virgin Mary)
b. Christ was God's manifestation on Earth
c. Christ died as the atonement for our sins
d. Christ was resurrected in his bodily form

25. Of the following, which statement about the US economy in the 1990s is correct?

a. By the year 2000, the US economy was increasing at a rate of 5% a year.
b. The rate of unemployment in America at this time dropped to 6%.
c. The rates of productivity and of inflation in the US were about the same.
d. The US stock market's total value had doubled in only six years.

26. In 20th-century America, which of the following occurred first?

a. The Emergency Quota Act was passed by Congress.
b. European immigration peaked at almost 1.3 million.
c. Congress passed a very restrictive Immigration Act.
d. The Great Depression caused decreased immigration.

27. Of the following events, which had an impact or was associated with the "New Left" of protesting youth in the 1960s?

a. The organization of the Students for a Democratic Society (SDS)
b. The organization of the Berkeley Free Speech Movement at UC
c. The assassinations of Martin Luther King, Jr. and Bobby Kennedy
d. All of the above.

28. Which of the following is NOT a common characteristic of all early civilizations?

a. Agricultural surplus
b. Clear division of labor
c. A pictographic writing system
d. Population centers such as towns and cities

29. Which of the following rivers did NOT play an important role in the development of the earliest civilizations?

a. The Tiber River
b. The Yangtze River
c. The Euphrates River
d. The Nile River

30. "The king allowed the conquered the right to maintain their own religious practices, local laws, and customs. This practice, however, shares no similarities with our present-day principals of tolerance. In effect, allowing conquered people to maintain their own religions and customs forged a bond of loyalty between the conqueror and the conquered. Though the conquered preserved many rights and customs, local governors called Satraps, along with a network of spies, maintained order and reported back to the King."

Which empire does the above passage describe?

a. Persians
b. Akkadians
c. Babylonians
d. Egyptians

31. Which of these factors did NOT contribute to the escalation of the Peloponnesian Wars?

a. Athens had amassed great power, which threatened other Greek city-states.
b. Athens had created a monopoly on sea trade in the region.
c. Several city-states formed an alliance with Sparta to keep Athens's power in check.
d. Athens invaded Sparta.

32. According to tradition, who founded the Hebrew people?

a. Zoroaster
b. Abraham
c. Aeneas
d. Daniel

33. Which of the following was NOT developed by the Phoenicians?

a. Purple dye
b. Sailing technology
c. The alphabet
d. The ziggurat

34. The first coin-based economy was established by which of the following people?

a. Phoenicians
b. Egyptians
c. Hebrews
d. Lydians

35. Which of the following choices is NOT true about early Christian monasticism?

a. At first, all monks were hermits modeled on St. Anthony the Great.
b. Pachomius organized his followers into the first monastery in 318.
c. Basil the Great in the West, and Benedict in the East, were leaders.
d. The rule of St. Benedict was the most common of medieval rules.

36. The Renaissance which began in Italy subsequently spread to which of the following other countries in Europe?

a. England
b. France
c. Germany
d. All of these

37. Which of the following statements does NOT characterize the Age of Absolutism?

a. Nobles gained more power as monarchs had them live in their palaces.
b. The influence of the Church upon government diminished at this time.
c. The partitioning characteristic of feudal systems no longer took place.
d. All of these were characteristics found during the Age of Absolutism.

38. Which of the following is NOT true about the English Civil Wars between 1641 and 1651?

a. These wars all were waged between Royalists and Parliamentarians.
b. The outcome of this series of civil wars was victory for Parliament.
c. These wars legalized Parliament's consent as requisite to monarchy.
d. Two of the wars in this time involved supporters of King Charles I.

39. Which of the following is a correct statement regarding consequences of the French Revolution?

a. De Tocqueville wrote that it showed the rising middle class's growing self-awareness.
b. Conservative Edmund Burke felt it was a minority conspiracy with no valid claims.
c. Marxists viewed it as a huge class struggle with lower and middle classes revolting.
d. All of these statements are correct regarding consequences of the French Revolution.

40. "I will never accept any proposals that will obligate the Jewish people to leave France, because to me the Jews are the same as any other citizen in our country. It takes weakness to chase them out of the country, but it takes strength to assimilate them." Who said this?

a. Maximilien Robespierre
b. Napoleon Bonaparte (I)
c. Marquis de La Fayette
d. The Abbé E. J. Sieyès

41. Which of these is NOT true relative to the rise of Fascism in Europe?

a. Fascism was opposed to nationalism and to patriotism.
b. Fascism was opposed to Marxism and the bourgeoisie.
c. Fascism purported to be an alternative to Bolshevism.
d. Fascism had some things in common with Bolshevism.

42. Which of the following is NOT a true statement about the Second World War?

a. It was a war wherein nations mobilized civilian as well as military resources.
b. It was a war wherein nations destroyed civilian as well as military personnel.
c. It eventually became known as "The War to End All Wars."
d. It was the first war in history to detonate nuclear devices.

43. Of the following countries, which did NOT experience more war soon after World War II?

a. Greece
b. China
c. Korea
d. Japan

44. Decolonization was difficult or impossible in countries with large, long-term settler populations where the settler population was too important and/or the indigenous population had become a minority. Of the following countries, which one had a settler population that moved out and relocated upon the country's decolonization?

a. The Chinese population of Singapore
b. The large Jewish population of Algeria
c. The British population of Cayman Islands
d. The Russian population of Kazakhstan

45. Of the following statements, which was NOT a characteristic of the Nuclear Age in the 1950s?

a. The 1950s were a decade of nuclear optimism, as nuclear power was seen in a positive light.
b. While almost everything was expected to become atomic, cars were not yet included.
c. People expected that the atomic bomb would replace all other earlier kinds of explosives.
d. Nuclear power was expected to replace all other energy sources such as coal or oil.

46. Which of the following statements is NOT true of the hierarchy of the Catholic Church?

a. Parish priests make up a diocese.
b. The head of the diocese is called a bishop.
c. The archdiocese is a collection of smaller dioceses overseen by the archbishop.
d. The curia is a group of archbishops with power over the pope.

47. Which of the following terms describes the practice of ostracizing Catholics who did not believe in official church policies or doctrines?

a. Heretics
b. Excommunication
c. Interdict
d. Canon Law

48. Which of the following was NOT a cause of the first Crusade?

a. The Turks overtook Jerusalem in 1065.
b. 3,000 Christian pilgrims were massacred in Jerusalem.
c. Turks threatened to invade Constantinople.
d. There was a desire to distract the public from the abuse of power seen during the Inquisition.

49. "Before his religious conversion, he persecuted Jews who converted to Christianity. After experiencing a religious vision, he became the early Christian church's strongest proponent, founding and counseling churches throughout Greece and Macedonia. These churches went on to form the foundation of the religion that would eventually spread throughout the Roman Empire."

The above passage describes which of the men below?

a. Jesus
b. Paul
c. Peter
d. David

50. Which of the following statements is NOT true about slavery in America?

a. The Spanish brought African slaves to Florida by the 1560s.
b. Chattel (ownership) slavery was legal in America from 1654 to 1865.
c. Indentured servants preceded slavery in America as sources of labor.
d. Southern colonies imported more slaves in the 1600s to farm cotton.

51. Which of the following is NOT correct concerning the Articles of Confederation?

a. They established the confederation's name as The United States of America.
b. They gave one vote apiece to each state in the Congress of the Confederation.
c. They established the freedom, sovereignty, and equality of individual states.
d. They gave individual states the sovereign right to wage war using state militias.

52. The legislative structure set forth in the US Constitution was determined by:

a. The Virginia Plan
b. The New Jersey Plan
c. The Connecticut Compromise
d. The Plan of Charles Pinckney

53. Which of the following is NOT true about the United States Constitution?

a. It is the oldest written constitution still used by any country today.
b. Its first thirteen amendments make up the Bill of Rights document.
c. It is the shortest written constitution still used by any nation today.
d. It replaced the Articles of Confederation after a period of six years.

54. What federal agency was created as an outcome of World War I?

a. The Food Administration
b. The Fuel Administration
c. Railroad Administration
d. All of the above

55. "This era represents the golden age of the Roman Empire. For about 200 years, the Empire experienced relatively few attacks, stability among its conquered lands, and significant developments in architecture and the engineering of roads and bridges. This time period saw the greatest expansion of the empire and the Romanization of the western world."

The above passage refers to which era of Roman history?

a. The reign of Julio-Claudian line of emperors
b. The reign of the Five Good Emperors
c. Pax Romana
d. The reign of the Flavian Emperors

56. What are common social demographics for liberals?

a. Single, religious, and educated
b. Single, secular, and educated
c. Married, religious, and educated
d. Married, secular, and gun owners

57. Virginian ____________ advocated a stronger central government and was influential at the Constitutional Convention.

a. Benjamin Franklin
b. James Madison
c. George Mason
d. Robert Yates

58. What are the first ten amendments to the Constitution more commonly known as?

a. The Civil Rights Act
b. Common law
c. The Equal Protection clause
d. The Bill of Rights

59. What percentage of votes does the Senate need to pass a bill?

a. Two-thirds majority
b. A simple majority
c. A supermajority
d. Three-quarters majority

60. The vice president succeeds the president in case of death, illness or impeachment. What is the order of succession for the next three successors, according to the Presidential Succession Act of 1947?

a. President pro tempore of the Senate, secretary of state, and secretary of defense
b. Speaker of the House, president pro tempore of the Senate, and secretary of state
c. President pro tempore of the Senate, Speaker of the House, and secretary of state
d. Secretary of state, secretary of defense, and Speaker of the House

61. The President has the power to veto legislation. How is this power limited?

I. Congress can override the veto
II. The President cannot line veto
III. The President cannot propose legislation

a. I and III
b. II only
c. I and II
d. I only

62. The president serves as commander-in-chief. What are the president's two limitations in that role?

a. The president cannot declare war or make rules governing the military.
b. The president cannot enforce blockades or declare war.
c. The president cannot enforce quarantines or make rules governing the military.
d. The president cannot enforce blockades or quarantines.

63. Disagreements between individuals or organizations are tried in:

a. Civil court
b. Criminal court
c. Federal court
d. State court

64. What best describes the way Washington, D.C. is governed?

a. Congress has ultimate authority.
b. Washington, D.C. has a local government similar to that of other cities in the area.
c. There is no local government in place.
d. There is a mayor and city council, but Congress has the authority to overrule their decisions.

65. The Political Affairs Agency is part of which department?

a. The Department of State
b. The Department of Defense
c. The Department of Homeland Security
d. The Department of Security

66. All of the Cabinet members have the title Secretary EXCEPT:

a. The head of the Department of Agriculture
b. The head of the Department of Justice
c. The head of the Department of Commerce
d. The head of the Department of Defense

67. Which Supreme Court case enforced the civil rights of citizens to not incriminate themselves?

a. Marbury v. Madison
b. Miranda v. Arizona
c. Youngstown Sheet and Tube Company v. Sawyer
d. United States v. Carolene Products Company

68. What do the American labor union movement, the antislavery movement, the women's suffrage movement, and the civil rights movement all have in common?

a. They all used political protest.
b. They all appealed to legal precedent.
c. They all came from political homogeneity.
d. They were all protected by the commerce clause.

69. Who may write a bill?

a. Anyone
b. A member of the House
c. A Senator
d. Any member of Congress

70. To be President of the United States, one must meet these three requirements:

a. The President must be college educated, at least 30 years old, and a natural citizen.
b. The President must be a natural citizen, have lived in the US for 14 years, and have a college education.
c. The President must be a natural citizen, be at least 35 years old, and have lived in the US for 14 years.
d. The President must be at least 30 years old, be a natural citizen, and have lived in the US for 14 years.

71. The president may serve a maximum of _____ according to the ___ Amendment.

a. Three four-year terms; 23rd
b. Two four-year terms; 22nd
c. One four-year term; 22nd
d. Two four-year terms; 23rd

72. The Office of Management and Budget helps the President prepare the federal budget. What is it a part of?

a. United States Trade Agency
b. Federal Reserve Board
c. Securities and Exchange Commission
d. Executive Office of the President

73. What effect do minor political parties have on the elections?

a. They are too small to threaten major parties.
b. They take funding away from major parties.
c. They often work with the major parties.
d. They can potentially take votes away from major parties.

74. Which of the following statements about special interest groups is true?

a. Special interest groups often utilize email and mass media.
b. Business groups generally favor Republican candidates.
c. Special interest groups often file amicus curiae briefs in cases in which they are not directly involved.
d. All of these are true.

75. What is a committee that raises money for political candidates and is formed by business, labor, or other special interest groups?

a. Party
b. Lobby
c. PLEO
d. PAC

76. People are typically made aware of political culture, facts, and values through family, friends, society, and:

a. Media
b. Census takers
c. History
d. Gun ownership

77. How do the media and public opinion or polls influence one another?

a. The media does not affect polls or public opinion.
b. The media is unbiased and simply presents candidates.
c. The way the media presents a candidate affects polls, and polls influence media portrayal.
d. The media controls poll results.

78. What was an early difference between Marxism and fascism?

a. Fascism came out of socialism and Marxism from capitalism.
b. Fascists were nationalists and Marxists had an international focus.
c. Fascists wanted to defeat capitalism and Marxists wanted to preserve private property.
d. Marxism originally wanted to preserve class structure and fascism supported capitalism.

79. What does NOT help ensure a two-party system?

a. A winner-take-all system
b. A proportional representative system
c. State and federal laws
d. Political culture

80. How did the attacks of 2001 directly influence American patriotic sentiment?

a. The attacks in 2001 both increased and decreased American patriotic sentiment in different populations.
b. The attacks in 2001 primarily decreased American patriotic sentiment.
c. The attacks in 2001 did not have a large effect on American patriotic sentiment.
d. The attacks in 2001 primarily increased American patriotic sentiment.

81. Which supranational institution regulates international trade, human rights, and nation development?

a. The UN
b. The EEOC
c. The UNDP
d. The GOP

82. Antarctica will appear the largest on a

a. Mercator projection
b. Robinson projection
c. Homolosine projection
d. Azimuthal projection

83. Tracy needs to determine the shortest route between Lima and Lisbon. Which of the following maps should she use?

a. Azimuthal projection with the North Pole at the center
b. Azimuthal projection with Lisbon at the center
c. Robinson projection of the Eastern Hemisphere
d. Robinson projection of the Western Hemisphere

84. During which stage of spatial diffusion does the process slow to a stop?

a. Primary
b. Diffusion
c. Condensing
d. Saturation

85. On which of the following maps would the scale be largest?

a. A map of Benelux nations
b. A map of Senegal
c. A map of Rio de Janeiro
d. A map of Greenwich Village

86. Which of the following is a possible absolute location for New Orleans?

a. 30° S, 90° E
b. 30° N, 90° E
c. 30° S, 90° W
d. 30° N, 90° W

87. Which of the following is NOT a method of representing relief on a physical map?

a. Symbols
b. Color
c. Shading
d. Contour Lines

Refer to the following for question 88:

A biome featuring scrubby plants and small evergreen trees has a hot, dry summer followed by a wetter winter. The following food chain exists in the biome:

$$tree \rightarrow caterpillar \rightarrow frog \rightarrow snake \rightarrow hawk \rightarrow vulture \rightarrow worm$$

88. Which biome is this?

a. Taiga
b. Coniferous forest
c. Chaparral
d. Savanna

89. In the plate movement known as ____, an oceanic plate slides underneath a continental plate.

a. faulting
b. spreading
c. subduction
d. converging

90. Which of the following statements about tropical rain forests is false?

a. There are tropical rain forests on only two continents.
b. The largest tropical rain forest is the Amazon River basin.
c. Over half of the world's plant and animal species are found in the tropical rain forest.
d. Tropical rain forests cover less than 10 percent of the earth's surface.

91. Which of the following locations would be considered a modern cultural hearth?

a. New York City
b. Baghdad
c. Auckland
d. Edmonton

92. Juan has a mill, which he uses to grind wheat into flour. This is an example of

a. Primary economic activity
b. Secondary economic activity
c. Tertiary economic activity
d. Quaternary economic activity

93. In the United States, what is the correct term for a settlement with fewer than 100 inhabitants?

a. Village
b. Town
c. Hamlet
d. City

94. When a person grows only enough food to feed himself and his family, he is engaged in

a. Nomadic herding
b. Commercial farming
c. Sharecropping
d. Subsistence farming

95. The popularity of hockey in Canada and the northern United States is an example of

a. Expansion diffusion
b. Indirect diffusion
c. Forced diffusion
d. Direct diffusion

96. During one year in Grassley County, there are 750 births, 350 deaths, 80 immigrations, and 50 emigrations. What is the natural increase rate for this year?

a. 400
b. 830
c. 430
d. More information is required.

97. Which form of religion includes the belief that the natural world is imbued with spirits?

a. Monotheism
b. Pantheism
c. Animism
d. Polytheism

98. Which of the following is NOT one of the criteria for nationhood?

a. Defined territory
b. Elections
c. Government
d. Sovereignty

99. When a foreign power has some political and economic control over a region in another country but does not directly govern, it is said to have a(n)

a. Colony
b. Sphere of Influence
c. Settlement
d. Enclave

100. Which of the following nations is NOT a member of OPEC?

a. Saudi Arabia
b. Venezuela
c. Yemen
d. Iraq

101. Which of the following statements concerning choice theory are correct?

I. Scarcity forces people, including producers, to make choices
II. Producers make choices and, as a result, face trade-offs
III. Opportunity cost is one way to measure the cost of a choice

a. I only
b. I and II only
c. II and III only
d. I, II, and III

102. A society produces 10 units of Good X and 10 units of Good Y. Then, the society changes its production, increasing production of Good X to 15 units. Production of Good Y drops to 6 units. What is the opportunity cost of producing the additional 5 units of Good X?

a. 5 units of Good X
b. 15 units of Good X
c. 6 units of Good Y
d. 4 units of Good Y

103. How is the long-run Phillips curve different than the short-run Phillips curve?

a. In the long-run Phillips curve, there is a trade-off between unemployment and inflation.
b. In the long-run Phillips curve, unemployment is always greater than inflation.
c. In the long-run Phillips curve, there is no trade-off between unemployment and inflation.
d. In the long-run Phillips curve, unemployment equals inflation.

104. Which of the following will result if two nations use the theory of comparative advantage when making decisions of which goods to produce and trade?

a. Each nation will make all of their own goods.
b. Both nations will specialize in the production of the same specific goods.
c. Each nation will specialize in the production of different specific goods.
d. Neither nation will trade with one another.

105. Which of the following are true of the demand curve?

I. It is normally downward sloping
II. It is normally upward sloping
III. It is influenced by the law of diminishing marginal utility
IV. It is unaffected by the law of diminishing marginal utility

a. I and III only
b. I and IV only
c. II and III only
d. II and IV only

106. The government increases spending by $1,000,000 and the multiplier is 5. How does this affect aggregate demand (AD)?

a. It has no effect.
b. AD will increase by $5,000,000.
c. AD will increase by $200,000.
d. AD will decrease by $5,000,000.

107. Which of the following statements is NOT true?

a. If the government imposes a tax on a good, the supply curve will shift to the left.
b. If the government imposes a tax on a good, it will result in a deadweight loss.
c. If the government imposes a tax on a good with a highly inelastic demand, it will be difficult for producers of the good to shift the cost to consumers.
d. If the government imposes a tax on a good, the market price of the good will likely increase.

108. The price of gasoline skyrockets, dramatically affecting the amount that producers spend to send their goods to market. What do you expect to happen in the short run?

a. Prices increase, GDP increases
b. Prices decrease, GDP decreases
c. Prices increase, GDP decreases
d. Prices decrease, GDP increases

109. Which of the following is NOT true of monopolistic competition?

a. There are no great barriers to entry or exit from the market.
b. Firms within monopolistic competition benefit from product differentiation.
c. Firms within monopolistic competition maximize profit by producing where MR = MC.
d. Firms in monopolistic competition are efficient.

110. The value of a "market basket" of goods and services in one year compared to the value of the same goods and services in another year is known as what?

a. CPI
b. GDP
c. GNP
d. CCI

111. Which of the following statements about the long run aggregate supply (LRAS) curve is correct?

a. The horizontal part represents high levels of unemployment.
b. The curved part represents high levels of unemployment.
c. The vertical part represents high levels of unemployment.
d. The LRAS curve is a straight, vertical line.

112. Assume the Fed acts to try to keep rising prices stable. Which theory suggests that unemployment will increase as a result?

a. Phillips curve
b. Business cycle
c. Circular flow model
d. Classical economics

113. Which of the following is most likely to benefit from inflation?

a. A bond investor who owns fixed-rate bonds
b. A retired widow with no income other than fixed Social Security payments
c. A person who has taken out a fixed-rate loan
d. A local bank who has loaned money out at fixed rate

114. Which of the following would be most likely to try to combat inflation by decreasing the money supply?

a. A believer in the Laffer Curve
b. A supply-side economist
c. A Keynesian economist
d. An advocate of monetary policy

115. Assume that the loanable funds market is at equilibrium at the intersection of Id_{m1} and S. Then, the US government raises taxes on corporations. At which point is equilibrium established?

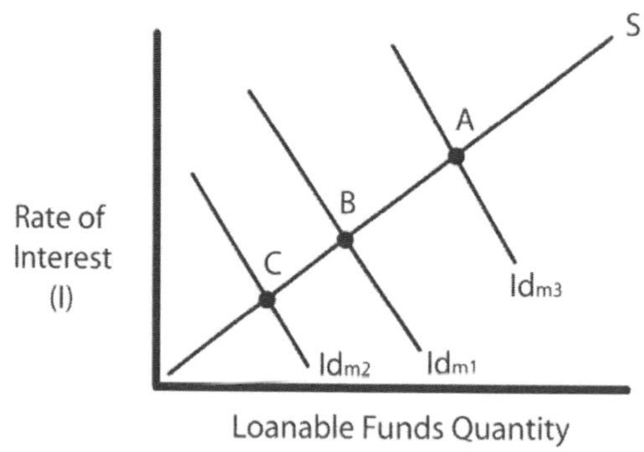

a. A
b. B
c. C
d. Some point above S

116. A business takes out a one-year loan to pay for an investment on January 1. On December 31 of that year they pay the loan back. During that time, the nation experiences a recession, and the overall price level in the economy drops. Which of the following statements is true?

a. The nominal interest rate of the loan is greater than the real interest rate.
b. The real interest rate of the loan is greater than the nominal interest rate.
c. The nominal interest rate of the loan is greater than the nominal rate.
d. The loan has a real interest rate but not a nominal rate.

117. The value of the goods and services exported by a country within a year and the goods and services imported by that same country during the same year is captured most directly in what?

a. Balance of payments
b. Current account
c. Capital account
d. Financial account

118. An increase in the value of the American dollar in foreign exchange markets might be caused by what?

a. An increase in aggregate demand (AD) in the US
b. An increase in interest rates in the US
c. A balance of payments that equals zero (debits equal credits)
d. Inflation in the US

119. What must nominal GDP be multiplied by to arrive at real GDP?

a. GNP
b. Price Deflator
c. Supply
d. Demand

120. The best definition of culture is:

a. The actual expression of societal norms
b. The ideal of what should occur in a particular society
c. The universal practices evident in all societies
d. The sum of everything learned by participants in a society

121. Which of the following best characterizes ethnocentrism?

a. The belief that one's personal culture is superior to others
b. The idea that it is difficult to adapt to a new culture
c. The idea that some cultures pre-date others
d. The belief that matriarchal societies are superior

122. If a man is concurrently described as being a psychologist, a husband, a father, and a respected member of the community, he is being defined according to his:

a. Ascribed status
b. Master status
c. Achieved status
d. Status set

123. Sociocultural evolution:

a. Describes the inclination of cultures to increase in complexity in the long run
b. Describes the interconnection which exists between people
c. Describes the quantity of cultural elements which are environmentally based
d. Describes a specific method of categorizing societies

124. The sociologist who defines modern conflict theory according to educational credentials is:

a. Karl Marx
b. Randall Collins
c. Ralf Dahrendorf
d. Max Weber

125. An illustration of the emergent-norm theory in action is:

a. An adult shoots a thief, and others fire their own shots shortly thereafter
b. A crowd storms through town to defend a wounded soldier
c. A father becomes threatened because his son is more successful than he is
d. A child attempts to convince a group that violence is wrong

126. __________ is the study of how the different parts of the body interact with one another and how this communication affects behavior.

a. Behavioral neuroscience
b. Behaviorism
c. Humanism
d. All of the above are correct

127. Johnny loves soccer and wants to join the soccer team. Though he does not particularly like football, his parents press him to join the football team. Johnny ends up joining the football team in order to please his parents. This is an example of:

a. Conditions of worth
b. Ideal self
c. Morality principle
d. Reality principle

128. Jesse struggled with depression one summer. His mother began to bring him breakfast in bed every day to cheer him up. Jesse began sleeping in even longer. When he did get up, he kept completely to himself. The more Jesse withdrew, the more his mother showered him with attention and gifts. This explanation of abnormal behavior comes from which of the following perspectives?

a. Cognitive approach
b. Learning or behavioral approach
c. Medical approach
d. Psychoanalytic approach

129. __________ was responsible for a famous experiment in which teachers were told to administer an electrical shock to students every time a student gave a wrong answer.

a. Solomon Asch
b. Kitty Genovese
c. Karen Horney
d. Stanley Milgram

130. _________ was a woman who was raped and killed in 1964 while thirty-eight witnesses watched. The witnesses did not call the police until after the killer was gone.

a. Virginia E. Johnson
b. Kitty Genovese
c. Karen Horney
d. Lana Brock

Answer Key and Explanations for Test #1

1. B: The Aztec was a Mesoamerican civilization of the pre-Columbian period. The Aztecs were ethnic groups of central Mexico dominant in large areas of Mesoamerica in the 14th-16th centuries. The Inca (A) was an Andean civilization from Peru. The Incas had the largest pre-Columbian empire, including Peru and major parts of Argentina, Bolivia, Chile, Colombia, and Ecuador in the 15th and 16th centuries. The Moche (C) was an Andean civilization in northern Peru between 100 and 800; this civilization is known for their artworks, architecture, and irrigation systems. They built the Huaca del Sol, an adobe pyramid that was the largest pre-Columbian construction in Peru before the Conquistadores destroyed part of it. The Cañaris (D) was an Andean tribe living in the south central part of Ecuador. The Incas eventually conquered the Cañaris, but the Cañaris resisted this conquest for many years. They were also known for their architecture, which had many Incan influences. They existed until their main city, Tumebamba, was destroyed by Atahualpa during the Inca Civil War in the 16th century.

2. C: The Pilgrims were not Puritans seeking to escape religious persecution in England. They were actually English Separatists (D) who believed there was no fixing the Church of England, and thus chose to separate from it. They did embark on the *Mayflower* in 1620, and storms drove the ship to land at Cape Cod, Massachusetts (A). Their leader was William Bradford, and they had been given a charter by the London Company to settle America (B) south of the Hudson River.

3. D: It is not true that Colonel Nicols granted very few civil or political rights to New York colonials. In fact, he gave them as many civil and political rights as possible to make up for the fact that James, Duke of York, who conquered New Amsterdam with his brother King Charles II's authorization (B), was strongly against representation for colonists, and prohibited any representative assemblies in his renamed New York (C). James gave in to their demands in the 1680s, but upon his accession to the throne of England in 1685, he went back on his word. It is true that before the English conquered the New York territories, New Amsterdam on Manhattan Island was a trading settlement of the New Netherlands made by Dutch explorers to facilitate the Dutch West India Company's fur trade with the indigenous peoples (A).

4. A: Women settlers outnumbering male settlers was not something that contributed to the differences between life in the New England colonies and life in the Chesapeake colonies. It was the other way around - in Virginia and Maryland, men greatly outnumbered women due to these colonies' large tobacco farms, which required men as workers. New England colonists did have life expectancies that were between 15 and 20 years longer than did Chesapeake colonists (B). Because Puritans lived longer, came to America with their families (most Chesapeake colonists came as individual indentured servants), and were a more homogeneous population, society in colonial New England was better organized and more stable than in the Chesapeake colonies (C). Puritans were also great believers in literacy because they felt it was so important to be able to read the Bible, so they had educational advantages over the colonies to the south (D). Because of the disproportionate sex ratio and the shorter life spans of Chesapeake settlers, their family and social lives were not as continuous or as stable as in New England. A combination of smaller farms, cottage industries, trading, fishing and ship building industries, and the resulting emergence of Boston as a chief international seaport all contributed to local prosperity in New England.

5. D: The conquistadores had to deal with labor shortages during their colonization of America in the 16th century. To address the shortage of labor, the Spanish first used Indian slaves. Only after the Indians were decimated by diseases brought from Europe and from being overworked did the

Spanish begin to import slaves from Africa (B). The first system used by the Spanish was the *encomienda* system of large estates or manors, which was only later succeeded by the *hacienda* system (C), which was similar but not as harsh. It is not true that New Spain's society had no kind of class system (A). In fact, this society was rigidly divided into three strata. The highest class was Spanish natives (*peninsulares*), the middle class consisted of those born in America to Spanish parents (*creoles*), and the lowest class was made up of Mestizos, or Indians.

6. D: General William Howe (A), General Henry Clinton (B), and General John Burgoyne (C) were all British generals who came to Boston in May of 1775 to push General Gage to pursue further aggression against Americans.

7. D: Ethan Allen (A) and Benedict Arnold (B) led the troops that captured Fort Ticonderoga in May of 1775. Following this victory, on December 31 of 1775, General Richard Montgomery (C) led an expedition to Montreal and Quebec to try to enlist the aid of Canada in America's resistance to Britain. This expedition met with another expedition led by Benedict Arnold. Their assault on Quebec was not successful. Montgomery was killed and Arnold was wounded.

8. C: The earliest event was the Second Continental Congress issuing the "Declaration of the Causes and Necessity for Taking up Arms" and sending the "Olive Branch Petition" to King George III, begging him to make peace with the American colonies. This took place in May of 1775. Following this, the King ignored the request for peace and approved the Prohibitory Act, declaring America to be in rebellion and thus not protected by him (D). This also took place in 1775. The next event chronologically in this list was (B). Thomas Paine published *Common Sense* in January of 1776, which urged Americans to vie immediately for independence from England. On July 4, 1776, (A) America's Second Continental Congress officially accepted the Declaration of Independence.

9. C: James Madison was the one who designed the Virginia Plan. Edmund Randolph, a more proficient public speaker, introduced this plan at Madison's request—not the other way around. It is true that the Convention delegates believed that humans are basically selfish by nature (A), which was why they instituted checks and balances in the constitution to keep the government or any part of it from abusing its powers or acquiring too much power. Benjamin Franklin was instrumental in the Great Compromise (B), which was reached with his help after the convention went into deadlock over choosing the Virginia Plan or the New Jersey Plan. The New Jersey Plan, designed by William Paterson, was offered as an alternative to the Virginia Plan (D), as it would give smaller states equal influence as larger states. The Great Compromise incorporated elements of both plans by having the equal representation outlined in the New Jersey Plan in the Senate and the representation based on population outlined in the Virginia Plan in the House of Representatives.

10. B: Hamilton did not object to US western expansionism, and Burr did not support it. There were certain Federalists other than Hamilton who opposed expansion to the west as a threat to their position within the Union, and these opponents did attempt to organize a movement to secede (A). To get Aaron Burr to champion their cause, they offered to help him run for Governor of New York (C). Hamilton did lead the opposition against Burr's campaign (D).

11. D: The Erie Canal was officially opened on October 26, 1825, and connected the Hudson River to Lake Erie. The Cayuga-Seneca Canal (A), connecting the Erie Canal to Cayuga Lake and Seneca Lake, was first used in 1828. The Chambly Canal (B) is a Canadian canal in Quebec that was opened in 1843. It is not a part of the New York State Canal System, as the other canals listed here are. The Oswego Canal (C), which connects the Erie Canal to Lake Ontario at Oswego, was opened in 1828. In 1992, the New York State Barge Canal was renamed the New York State Canal System, which incorporates all of the canals listed in this question except for the Chambly Canal (B), which is not in New York State.

12. D: The written works Thomas Paine published *after* the American Revolution (1765-1783) were both *Rights of Man* and *The Age of Reason*. His *Rights of Man* (B) was published in 1791 in response to Edmund Burke's pamphlet *Reflections on the Revolution in France*, which criticized the French Revolution. Paine's *Rights of Man* defended the French Revolution. *The Age of Reason* (C) was a book Paine published in 1793-1794, which advocated deism and rationalism while criticizing traditional Christian beliefs and institutionalized religions. *Common Sense (A)* was a pamphlet Paine published in 1776, which was widely read and very influential to the American Revolution. Paine also published a series of pro-revolutionary pamphlets from 1776-1783 entitled *The American Crisis.*

13. D: It is not true that the Second Great Awakening's individualistic nature contradicted nationalism and expansionism. While it did have an individualistic nature, this evangelical movement, which started in 1801 at the first camp meeting in Cane Ridge, Kentucky, also created significant nationalistic feelings. These later resurfaced in the expansionist beliefs of Manifest Destiny. Therefore, the Second Great Awakening actually influenced nationalism and expansionism rather than contradicting them. In fact, the social implications of the Second Great Awakening later helped to ignite the major reform movements of the 1830s and 1840s. This movement was definitely a reaction to Enlightenment's focus on rationalism (A), and it did emphasize a type of religious faith that was individual, personal, and emotional (B). Women (C) participated in this movement in large numbers.

14. D: All of the statements regarding movements for reform in 1840s America are true. This was a period of change in society, meaning that conditions were unstable and people felt uncertainty (A). Additionally, many Americans during this time were challenging the old traditions and values (B). Romanticism began in Europe and spread to the New World as a reaction against the rationalism of the Enlightenment in both places. Romantics, preferring emotions over reason, had an optimistic belief in the basic goodness of humanity and in its ability to become better, which lent itself well to ideas of reform (C). The movements for reform during this time were centered in the Northeastern states, particularly in the New England states.

15. D: All of these are examples of urban violence in 1830s America. Political differences between Democrats and Whigs in New York City escalated into such violent fighting that the state militia was called in to subdue the disagreeing parties (A). Race riots broke out in New York City and Philadelphia during this decade (B). An angry mob in New York even went so far as to raid a Catholic convent in 1834 (C). All of these events were attributable to the very rapid influx of people to the cities, causing mob violence and street crime to grow out of control.

16. C: The first transcontinental railroad was finished in 1869 (C) on May 10. Construction on the railroad was begun in 1862 (A) but not completed until seven years later. After completion, economic depression prevented more railroad building until the 1890s (B). In 1865 (D), there were 35 000 miles of railroad track in the country; by 1890 (B), there were 200 000 miles. The first transcontinental railroad connected the Central Pacific Railroad, which began in Sacramento, California, to the Union Pacific Railroad, which began in Omaha, Nebraska, in Utah.

17. D: All of these laws prepared the US for entry into World War I. The National Defense Act of 1916 (A) expanded America's armed forces, and the Navy Act (B), also in 1916, expanded the US Navy. In that same year, the Revenue Act (C) created new taxes to finance the growth of America's military.

18. C: The earliest instance of Soviet-US differences was in 1945 when the USSR establishment of a communist government in Poland, which prohibited conservative participation (C). In 1947, the Soviets backed the Communist control of Hungary and Romania (A). In 1948, the Soviets also supported communist rule in Czechoslovakia (B). Later the USSR refused to participate in the Baruch Plan (D), which aimed to set up an international agency to manage the use of atomic energy. This action demonstrated an unwillingness to cooperate with other nations in the interest of peace. These events signified the beginning of the Cold War.

19. D: The 1961 Bay of Pigs invaders would best be described as Cuban exiles sponsored by the CIA. It was not members of the CIA themselves (A). It was a group of Cuban exiles (B), but this answer is not as correct as choice D, which further specifies that these Cuban exiles were sponsored by the CIA. They were also trained by the CIA and supported by US armed forces. The people of Cuba (C) did not invade nor did they support the invasion. In fact, the invasion was quashed by Cuban armed forces within three days.

20. A: Communists adhering to more traditional thought did stage a coup against Gorbachev, but it was not successful. Its failure proved the ineffectiveness of the Central Committee, the Communist Party, and the Soviet government. Gorbachev's actions at this time were not to preserve the communist union but to reform the government and the economy, and they ultimately led to the USSR dissolution. He initiated Perestroika, which, literally translated, means "restructuring," to reform the economy (B). He also instituted Glasnost, open government processes, to make Russian politics transparent to all (C), in an effort to decrease communist and Soviet government corruption. These new policies introduced by Gorbachev started a chain reaction of events in Eastern Europe that Soviets could not control. These included the collapse of East Germany's communist government in 1989, whereupon the Berlin Wall was dismantled, leading to East and West Germany's reunification in 1990 (D). In 1989, communist leadership ended in Poland, Hungary, Czechoslovakia, and Romania. In 1990, Bulgaria's and Albania's communist governments also fell, and that year Lithuania detached itself from the Soviet Union, at which point the Union fell apart. Following the failed coup attempt, the Soviet Union was dismantled.

21. D: Both answer A and answer C furthered the civil rights cause, but answer B impeded this cause. In the case of *Brown v. Board of Education of Topeka*, the Supreme Court's 1954 ruling stated that schools segregated by race are by nature not equal. This ruling was monumental in the NAACP's fight against school segregation. Orval Faubus, Governor of Arkansas, tried to prevent Little Rock High School's integration in 1957 (B). The situation escalated to the point that President Eisenhower nationalized the Arkansas National Guard and sent the 101st Airborne Division to protect the high school students from harm (C). These actions furthered civil rights by showing the government's defense of school integration.

22. D: The war ended during Nixon's administration, not during LBJ's term. The Great Society program included legislation to create Medicare (A), eliminate obstacles hindering the right to vote (B), provide federal funding for education (C), and establish the Department of Housing and Urban Development (HUD). The Great Society also included a number of programs aimed at alleviating poverty. Johnson's social reform accomplishments were overshadowed by the Vietnam War during his last two years in office.

23. A: It is not true that the US captured Osama bin Laden shortly after the attacks. On October 7, the US attacked the Taliban regime in Afghanistan and defeated it in November, so these events did occur shortly after September 11, 2001, but bin Laden was not captured and killed until nearly ten years later, on May 2, 2011. It is true that Muslim terrorists flew two of the four American airplanes they had hijacked into the twin towers of the World Trade Center in New York City (B). They flew the third of the four planes into the US Department of Defense's headquarters, the Pentagon building in Arlington, Virginia, (C) near Washington, D.C. The fourth plane crashed in a field near Shanksville, Pennsylvania, after some of the passengers on board tried to overtake the terrorists (D). President George W. Bush announced a "war on terrorism" after these attacks killed a total of 2,995 people.

24. B: The "five fundamentals" of the General Assembly of the Presbyterian Church in 1910 did not include the idea that Christ was God's manifestation on Earth. Although this is a common Christian concept, it was not one of the five fundamentals endorsed by Christian Fundamentalists. In addition to the idea that the Bible was inspired by the Holy Spirit and therefore true and/or infallible, the other four of the five fundamentals were that (A) Christ was born to a virgin; that (C) Christ's death was the atonement for sin; that (D) Christ was resurrected in his bodily form; and that Christ performed the miracles shown in the Bible. Within less than ten years after the Presbyterian assembly arrived at these five fundamentals, people who endorsed them came to be known as Fundamentalists.

25. C: The rates of both productivity and inflation in the US were approximately 2% by 2000. By this time, the US economy was not increasing at a rate of 5% a year (A) but of 4% a year. Almost half of industrial growth contributing to economic prosperity was due to the "information revolution" made possible by the invention of the PC. The rate of unemployment in America at this time had not gone down to 6% (B) but to 4.7%. The stock market in the US had not just doubled in six years (D); it had actually quadrupled from 1992-1998 due to the increase in American households that owned stocks or bonds. Most of this ownership resulted from tax law changes regulating retirement accounts.

26. B: European immigration to America, the first event, hit a high in 1907, when 1,285,349 European immigrants came to America. The numbers were so great that Congress passed the Emergency Quota Act (A) in 1921. In order to implement greater restrictions on the influx of Southern and Eastern Europeans—particularly Jews, Italians, and Slavs—arriving in larger numbers since the 1890s, and even more as refugees before and during the Nazi and World War II years, Congress further passed the 1924 Immigration Act (C), which prohibited most European refugees from entering the United States. During the Great Depression (D) of the 1930s, immigration declined sharply due to the lack of economic opportunities.

27. D: All of these (D) events were associated with and/or had an impact on the emergence of the New Left, young people who were politically and socially disenchanted with America. In 1962, in Port Huron, Michigan, the SDS (A), spearheaded by Tom Hayden, Alan Huber, and others, held its first convention and was subsequently instrumental in student organization and advocacy for social and political reform (until 1969). The Berkeley Free Speech Movement (B) was organized at the University of California at Berkeley by student Mario Savio and others, insisting that the university's administrators remove their ban on campus political activity and recognize students' rights to free speech. The student activism generated by the Free Speech movement continues to this day, albeit not as rampantly as at the movement's inception. In 1968, when first Martin Luther King Jr. and then Robert Kennedy, both major leaders for reform, were assassinated (C), young people were further disaffected.

28. C: Not all early civilizations developed a pictographic writing system. Though Egypt had a well-known pictographic writing system called hieroglyphs, other cultures used different forms of writing. For example, cuneiform is a language that does not use pictographs.

29. A: Roman civilization developed on the Tiber River, but it is not considered one of the earliest civilizations. Major civilizations developed along the other rivers listed: Chinese civilization developed in the Yangtze and Huang River valleys; Mesopotamian civilization emerged between the Tigris and Euphrates; and Egyptian culture developed in the Nile River valley.

30. A: The word "Satrap" is associated with Persian governors, not Akkadians, Babylonians, or Egyptians.

31. D: Athens did not invade Sparta. Athens' power did create resentment among other Greek city-states. Athens' monopoly on trade accounts for a significant cause of the war. Sparta did establish an alliance to counteract the power of Athens.

32. B: Abraham is considered the founder of the Hebrew tradition. Zoroaster is not directly associated with the Hebrew tradition. Aeneas is a character from Greek legends, sometimes associated with the founding of Rome. Though Daniel shaped the history of the Hebrew people and religion, he is not considered the founder.

33. D: Ziggurats are tall stair-stepped towers built by Mesopotamians. The remaining choices are all examples of Phoenician developments: the Phoenicians created purple dyes associated with royalty, sailing technology used all over the ancient world, and an alphabet which formed the foundation of many writing systems still in use, along with many other important inventions.

34. D: Around 600 BC, the Lydians of Asia Minor were one of the first to coin metal currency.

35. C: It is not true that Basil the Great was a leader in the West or that Benedict was a leader in the East with respect to early Christian monasticism. The reverse is true. St. Benedict was a leader of the monastic movement in the West, while Basil the Great was a monastic leader in the East. Initially, all monks were hermits, modeling their lifestyles on that of St. Anthony the Great (A). Eventually, perceiving the necessity of a spiritual organization, St. Pachomius created what would become the first monastery in 318 (B). St. Benedict created the code of spiritual practice, or rule, known as the Rule of St. Benedict, which became the most-followed rule during the middle ages (D).

36. D: All of these countries experienced their own Renaissances following the Italian Renaissance, which began in the cities of Florence and Siena and spread through Italy. From there the intellectual and cultural developments of the period spread to France from the late 15th to early 17th century, to Germany in the 15th and 16th centuries, and to England from the early 16th to early 17th century, as well as to the Netherlands in the 16th century, in a movement often known as the Northern Renaissance. This name distinguishes it from the original Italian Renaissance.

37. A: Nobles did not gain more power during the Age of Absolutism. Though the monarchs of that period often did require nobility to live in their royal palaces, this practice brought the nobility less power rather than more power, since it forced the nobles into dependence upon the monarchs for their income while officials of the state governed the noblemen's lands. In addition to the nobility, the Church also experienced a loss of influence (B) during this period as the monarch and the state gained more power, and state laws were developed. Partitioning common under the feudal system no longer took place (C) as most or all of the power was consolidated to the monarch. Since choice A was not a characteristic of the Age of Absolutism, choice D, all of these, is incorrect.

38. C: It is not true that the English Civil Wars between 1641 and 1651 legalized Parliament's consent as a requirement for a monarch to rule England. These wars did establish this idea as a precedent, but the later Glorious Revolution of 1688 actually made it legal that a monarch could not rule without Parliamentary consent. The wars from 1641–1651 were all fought between Royalists who supported an absolute monarchy and Parliamentarians who supported the joint government of a parliamentary monarchy (A). Parliament was the victor (B) in 1651 at the Battle of Worcester. As a result of this battle, King Charles I was executed, and King Charles II was exiled. In the first of these civil wars, from 1642-1646, and the second, from 1648-1649, supporters of King Charles I (D) fought against supporters of the Long Parliament.

39. D: All of these statements are correct regarding consequences of the French Revolution. French historian and political analyst Alexis de Tocqueville (famous for his book Democracy in America) saw the French Revolution as signifying the increasing social self-awareness of the middle class as it gained wealth (A). Conservative, anti-French Revolution philosopher and political theorist Edmund Burke believed that the Revolution was started by a small faction of conspirators who had no valid claims (B) for revolting and who brainwashed the public into subversive action against the status quo. Those persons who subscribe to Marxist philosophy focus on the rising up of the lower and middle working classes (C) against elite royalty who enjoyed unfair privileges.

40. B: This quotation was said by Napoleon Bonaparte (Napoleon I). While some have emphasized his desire to assimilate Jews so thoroughly into French society that their Jewish identity would disappear, nonetheless he did emancipate the Jews. Maximilien Robespierre (A) was an attorney who controlled the Committee of Public Safety and was a key figure during the Reign of Terror. He was arrested and executed in 1794. The Directory then ran the country for four years until it was superseded by the Consulate under Napoleon I. The Marquis de La Fayette (C), Gilbert du Motier, was the commander of the French National Guard (Garde Nationale) during the French Revolution. He was previously a general in the American Revolution. In France, he proposed the meeting of the Estates-General, was vice president of it, and submitted a draft of the French Declaration of the Rights of Man and of the Citizen. The Abbé Emmanuel Joseph Sieyès (D) was a French Roman Catholic abbot and one of the architects of the French Revolution. His pamphlet *What Is the Third Estate?* (1789) helped the Estates-General to become the National Assembly. In 1799, he started the coup d'état that allowed Napoleon I to assume power.

41. A: Fascism was not opposed to nationalism and patriotism. Fascism was a radical political movement that was nationalistic in character. In fact, Fascism opposed Marxism (B) because Fascists saw Marxism as anti-nationalist and anti-patriotic. Fascism was both collectivist and saw itself as patriotic. Fascists were also against the bourgeoisie (B) for their individualism, which was the opposite of collectivism. Fascism did purport to be an alternative to Bolshevism (C). Nonetheless, despite this, the Fascist movement did have several things in common with Bolshevism (D). For example, both political movements believed in a single-party state, in appealing to the proletariat, and in the ruling over the masses by an elite group.

42. C: It is not true that the Second World War came to be known as "The War to End All Wars." Although this appellation sounds more fitting to WWII, it was actually the description given to the First World War. Of course, at the time of WWI no one knew that WWII would take place, so at that time the phrase seemed a suitable designation. Moreover, world leaders then wanted to avoid another world war in the future and thereby formed the League of Nations to prevent such an occurrence. When this proved unsuccessful in preventing WWII, the United Nations was formed. WWI was the worst war the world had ever experienced at the time, but when WWII broke out, it was far worse than WWI. It is true that in the Second World War, nations mobilized all of their resources—both military and civilian (A), to the point that there was no more distinction between the two. This war also claimed many more civilian casualties and military casualties (B) than previous wars. Very large contributors to the great numbers of civilian casualties were the Holocaust, wherein millions of people including Jews, Catholics, Jehovah's Witnesses, Romani, Poles, Soviet POWs, Freemasons, homosexuals, and people with disabilities were killed. Further, the

Second World War was the first war in history to detonate nuclear devices (D), when the United States under President Harry S. Truman bombed Hiroshima and Nagasaki after Japan refused the unconditional surrender terms demanded by the Allies at Potsdam, Germany.

43. D: Japan did not experience more war soon after WWII. Japan not only had good economic recovery from the war, as some other nations did, but it also experienced tremendous economic growth. Within 40 years of the war's end, Japan boasted one of the world's strongest economies. Greece (A) experienced a civil war from 1946-1949 between the government's army and the Communist Party's army. China (B) went back to the civil war it had been fighting on and off since 1927, resuming the fighting from 1946 until 1950. Korea (C) began the Korean War in 1950 when North Korea invaded South Korea.

44. B: The country and population that moved out and relocated was the large population of Sephardic and Ashkenazi Jews in Algeria when that country became independent from France. The majority of these Algerian Jews evacuated Algeria and repatriated to France after the Second World War. The Chinese population in Singapore (A), the British population in Cayman Islands (C), and the Russian population in Kazakhstan (D) represent situations in which the longtime settler populations and the minority indigenous populations make decolonization impractical (even when the minority and majority are somewhat close in numbers).

45. B: Cars *were* included in the expectations of converting to atomic energy during the 1950s Nuclear Age. Not only were cars included in these projections, the Ford Motor Company actually presented a prototype of a nuclear-powered car, the Ford Nucleon Concept Car, in 1958. Although the model never went into production, the prototype and the concept remained as a symbol of the Nuclear Age. During the 1950s, the public attitude was one of nuclear optimism wherein nuclear power was viewed as overwhelmingly positive (A). People projected that in the future, the atomic bomb would take the place of all other earlier types of explosives (C). They also thought that nuclear power would replace the use of all other power sources such as coal and oil (D). People in 1950s America felt that nuclear power eventually would prove useful for almost everything, and that all applications of nuclear power would be beneficial.

46. D: Each statement describes the hierarchy of the Catholic Church except choice D: the curia is the group of archbishops who elect new popes, but once chosen, the pope is the ultimate authority.

47. B: Heretic is a term used to describe one who has been excommunicated. Interdict refers to the church's authority to keep entire regions from receiving the sacraments. Canon law refers to the code of law that governed the church.

48. D: Each of the choices is true except choice D: the Crusades (which ended in the 13th century) occurred before the Inquisition (which began in the 15th century).

49. B: Paul of Tarsus played one of the most significant roles in the development of the early Christian Church.

50. D: It is not true that cotton farming was the reason Southern colonies imported more slaves in the 1600s. Tobacco farming was the reason. Tobacco became a very successful cash crop at that time in the American colonies. Growing tobacco was extremely labor-intensive, so planters needed more laborers as tobacco became more popular and valuable. Cotton was grown in America by the end of the 16th century and increased around the end of the 18th century due to Eli Whitney's invention of the cotton gin in 1793. It is true that slaves were brought from Africa to Florida by the Spanish as early as the 1560s (A), although this practice became more widespread practice in the 1600s. Chattel slavery (meaning outright ownership of a person for that person's lifetime) was legal in America from 1654 until 1865 (B) when Lincoln's Emancipation Proclamation abolished it. Furthermore, indentured servants provided sources of labor in America before slaves (C). Early indentured servitude was not race based, as the modern concept of race did not begin until the 1700s. Indentured servants were people who were bonded into servitude for a period of several years, often as a result of poverty, after which they could gain their freedom. An eventual shortage of indentured servants led to the importation of slaves and the enslavement of some indentured servants of African descent. By the end of the 17th century, court rulings had confined American slavery to people of African descent.

51. D: The Articles of Confederation did formally establish the name of the United States of America (A) for the new confederation. They did allocate just one vote to each state in the Congress of the Confederation (B), to which each state could send two to seven delegates. They did state that the individual states would keep their sovereignty, freedom, and equality (C) with the government of the confederation, and would maintain "...every power, jurisdiction, and right, which is not by this Confederation expressly delegated." The Articles of Confederation were in favor of state militias, but stated that no individual state could form armies or navies, or engage in war, without the permission of Congress.

52. C: The Connecticut Compromise was the plan that finally determined how the states would be represented in the government. During the Constitutional Convention or Philadelphia Convention, delegates drafting the Constitution disagreed on this point. The Virginia Plan (A), proposed by the Virginia delegation based on James Madison's ideas, held that states should be represented in proportion to their population sizes. Accordingly, the Virginia Plan was called the "large states plan." William Paterson proposed the New Jersey Plan (B). The New Jersey delegation objected to the Virginia Plan, as proportional representation could give unfair advantages to bigger states like Virginia and crowd out smaller states like New Jersey. The New Jersey Plan was called the "small states plan." It was rejected by the convention but helped small states have their point heard. The Plan of Charles Pinckney (D) of South Carolina has fewer recorded details as Pinckney did not present a written copy, and only James Madison's notes about it remain. The Convention did not debate Pinckney's plan. The Connecticut Compromise (C), proposed by Robert Sherman, reached a balance between large and small states by stipulating the House of Representatives numbers would be in proportion to the states' populations while each state would have equal representation in the Senate, with two Senators. This combined elements of both the Virginia/large states and New Jersey/small states plans. It took delegates 42 days to agree to this conclusion, but the Connecticut Compromise finally resolved the issue of state representation.

53. B: It is not true about the US Constitution that its first thirteen amendments make up the Bill of Rights. The Bill of Rights consists of the first *ten* amendments to the Constitution. Furthermore, the United States Constitution is actually both the oldest (A) and the shortest (C) written constitution still used by any country in the world today. The Constitution replaced the Articles of Confederation after a period of six years (D). The Articles of Confederation were ratified in 1781, and the Constitution was ratified in 1787.

54. D: All of the agencies listed (D) were federal agencies formed in response to World War I, and the institution of said agencies expanded the American federal government. The Food Administration (A) oversaw distribution and pricing of food. The Fuel Administration (B) managed distribution, pricing, and use of fuel for transportation. The Railroad Administration (C) worked with issues of railway transportation. Additional federal agencies included the War Industries Board, the War Shipping Board, and the National War Labor Board.

55. C: The passage describes the 200-year period known as *Pax Romana.* Choice A is incorrect because the Julio-Claudian line held power in Rome for less than a century. Choice B refers to a succession of emperors that lasted less than one hundred years. The emperors in choice D only ruled from 69 AD to 96 AD.

56. B: Citizens who consider themselves to be liberal tend to be single, secular, and educated. Conservatives are more likely to be married, religious, and own a firearm. Most Americans do not consider themselves to be extreme liberals or extreme conservatives.

57. B: James Madison was a close friend of Thomas Jefferson and supported a stronger central government. George Mason and Robert Yates were both against expanding federal authority over the states. Benjamin Franklin was a proponent of a strong federal government, but he was from Massachusetts.

58. D: The Bill of Rights was drafted by Congress to limit the authority of the government and protect the rights of individual citizens from abuse by the federal government. It was the first document to detail the rights of private citizens.

59. B: While the Senate needs a two-thirds or supermajority vote to ratify treaties, only a simple majority is necessary to pass a bill or confirm the appointments of the President.

60. B: The Presidential Succession Act lists the Speaker of the House, president pro tempore of the Senate, and secretary of state next in succession after the vice president. However, anyone who succeeds as president must meet all of the legal qualifications.

61. C: The President has the power to veto legislation directly or use a pocket veto by not signing a bill within ten days after receiving it. Congress adjourns during this time period. A veto can be overridden if two-thirds of the House and the two-thirds of the Senate both agree. The President must veto a complete bill and does not have the authority to veto sections or lines.

62. A: The president of the United States serves as commander-in-chief, but the writers of the Constitution, who feared how authority was used by monarchs, limited the president's power in this role. The president cannot declare war or make rules governing the military, although presidents have traditionally authorized the use of force without war being declared.

63. A: Arbitration between organizations or individuals takes place in civil court. Civil trials are similar to criminal proceedings and require a jury. Both parties, however, can agree to let a judge decide the case.

64. D: Washington, D.C., as the US capitol, is a federal district. It has a local government in the form of a mayor and city council, but Congress has ultimate authority and can override the decisions made by the local government.

65. A: The Political Affairs Agency is part of the Department of State. The Department of State is an executive agency and the Political Affairs Agency is run by the Under Secretary who supervises the bureaus for Africa, East Asia and the Pacific, Europe and Eurasia, the Near East, South and Central Asia, the Western Hemisphere, International Organizations, and International Narcotics and Law Enforcement.

66. B: The title Attorney General is given to the head of the Justice Department while every other member of the Executive Cabinet has the title Secretary.

67. B: The Supreme Court ruled that statements made in interrogation are not admissible unless the defendant is informed of the right to an attorney and waives that right. The case of Miranda v. Arizona was consolidated with Westover v. United States, Vignera v. New York, and California v. Stewart.

68. A: America has a history of organized political protest dating back to the American Revolution. The right to peaceful protest is protected by the First Amendment. The American labor union movement, the antislavery movement, the women's suffrage movement, and the civil rights movement all used political protest to gain support for their causes.

69. A: Anyone may write a bill, but only a member of Congress can introduce a bill. The President often suggests bills. Bills can change drastically throughout the review process.

70. C: The President must be a natural citizen, be at least 35 years old, and have lived in the US for 14 years. There is no education requirement for becoming President. Truman did not have a college education, but most Presidents have had college degrees.

71. B: Most presidents have only served two terms, a precedent established by George Washington. Ulysses S. Grant and Theodore Roosevelt sought third terms; however, only Franklin D. Roosevelt served more than two terms. He served a third term and won a fourth, but died in its first year. The 22nd Amendment was passed by Congress in 1947 and ratified in 1951. It officially limited the president to two terms, and a vice president who serves two years as president only can be elected for one term.

72. D: The Office of Management and Budget is part of the Executive Office of the President (EOP). The EOP is a group of Presidential advisers and has been in place since Theodore Roosevelt. The President appoints members directly, but some positions like the Director of the Office of Management and Budget need Senate approval.

73. D: Minor parties often split from major parties and take voters with them. For example, Nader's Green Party was a spoiler in the 2000 election. Gore was down by 500 votes in Florida, and Nader had 100,000 votes in that state. The influence of minor parties on elections often forces the major parties to adjust their ideology.

74. D: All of these are true. Special interest groups utilize e-mail and mass media. They file amicus curiae briefs in cases that do not involve them directly. but the business sector usually favors Republican candidates due to the commonality of pro-business policies supported by Republicans.

75. D: Political Action Committees (PACs) raise money for political candidates and are formed by business, labor, or other special interest groups. They may donate $5,000 per candidate per election, but can contribute larger amounts for party-building activities.

76. A: Political socialization occurs when people are made aware of political culture, facts, and values. Family, friends, society, and the media influence political socialization. Sex, race, age, education, income, and region are also indicators of how a person will vote.

77. C: The way the media presents a candidate helps determine polls and public opinion. Candidates who the media presents favorably usually have better numbers in the polls, and candidates who are behind in the polls are often not presented favorably.

78. B: Fascism and Marxism both came out of socialism, and while they had some similarities, they did not support each other. Fascism was focused on specific nations, and Marxism focused on the working class of the world in an attempt to overthrow capitalism. Fascism sought to bring the private sector under government control while preserving private property and class divisions.

79. B: America has a history of a two-party system dating back to the Federalist and Anti-Federalists. Different laws, culture, and a winner-take-all system make it difficult for minor parties to gain ground. America does not have a proportional representative system where the percentage of the population that agrees with a party is directly represented.

80. D: Patriotic sentiment is support and devotion to one's nation. The word "nationalism" also refers to the support of one's own nation, often placing the support of one's own nation over worldwide interests. The terrorist attacks of 2001 had an immediate and direct effect of increasing feeling of patriotic sentiment, or nationalism, among US citizens. In the following years, continuous involvement of the US in the war, along with loss of lives, negative economic impact, and changes in national security policies have had a more periodic effect of decreasing patriotic or nationalistic sentiment. These changes in sentiment are more indirect and do not accurately depict the short-term surge of sentiment stemming from the terrorist attacks of 2001.

81. A: The UN is a supranational institution made up of participating nations that develop international laws. Recent globalization makes supranational institutions such as the UN, EU, and ECOWAS more influential in political policies.

82. A: Antarctica will appear the largest on a Mercator projection. This projection map converts the globe into a rectangle, such that lines of longitude and latitude are perpendicular to one another. This type of map depicts landforms near the equator at nearly their normal size but increasingly stretches out distances as it reaches the poles. A Robinson projection, on the other hand, rounds the edges of the Mercator projection, such that the polar regions are not so large. A homolosine projection renders the sizes and shapes of landmasses correctly, but it distorts the distances between them. An azimuthal projection represents one hemisphere as a circle, such that a straight line from the center to any point on the map would also be the shortest distance in the real world.

83. B: To determine the shortest route between Lima and Lisbon, Tracy should use an azimuthal projection with Lisbon at the center. An azimuthal projection depicts one hemisphere of the globe as a circle. A straight line drawn from the center of the map to any point represents the shortest possible distance between those two points. Tracy could obtain her objective, then, with an azimuthal projection in which either Lisbon or Lima were at the center. If the North Pole were at the center, the map would not include Lima because this city is in the Southern Hemisphere. A Robinson projection approximates the sizes and shapes of landmasses but does distort in some ways, particularly near the poles.

84. D: In the saturation stage of spatial diffusion, the process slows down and eventually stops altogether. The Swedish geographer Torsten Hägerstrand outlined four stages in spatial diffusion, which is the spread of innovation throughout a geographical region. In the primary stage, the innovation first appears and is adopted in the immediate vicinity. In the diffusion stage, the innovation is used in increasingly far-flung areas. In the condensing stage, any areas that had not already received the innovation do so. In the saturation stage, the innovation is either replaced or abandoned because it is no longer believed to have utility.

85. D: The scale would be largest on a map of Greenwich Village. Scale is described as large when it is closer to life-sized; the smaller the region being depicted, the closer to actual size the map can be. Of the four answer choices, Greenwich Village, a neighborhood in Manhattan, is the smallest.

Therefore, it must be depicted in the largest scale. Incidentally, Benelux is the name for the region of northern Europe that includes Belgium, the Netherlands, and Luxembourg.

86. D: The only answer choice that represents a possible absolute location for New Orleans is 30° N, 90° W. When a location is described in terms of its placement on the global grid, it is customary to put the latitude before the longitude. New Orleans is north of the equator, so it has to be in the Northern Hemisphere. In addition, it is west of the prime meridian, which runs through Greenwich, England, among other places. So, New Orleans must be in the Western Hemisphere. It is possible, then, to deduce that 30° N, 90° W is the only possible absolute location for New Orleans.

87. A: Symbols are not used to represent relief on a physical map. A physical map is dedicated to illustrating the landmasses and bodies of water in a specific region, so symbols do not provide enough detail. Color, shading, and contour lines, on the other hand, are able to create a much more complicated picture of changes in elevation, precipitation, etc. Changes in elevation are known in geography as relief.

88. C: The chaparral biome features scrubby plants and small evergreen trees and also has a hot, dry summer followed by a wetter winter. This biome is mainly found around the Mediterranean Sea, though there are also chaparrals in Australia, South Africa, and the American Southwest. The taiga is a colder biome found primarily in northern Europe and Asia. The vegetation of the taiga is mainly scattered stands of coniferous trees. A coniferous forest, meanwhile, is a warmer forest composed of trees that have needles and cones rather than leaves. These trees are better suited for a cold climate than are deciduous trees. A savanna is a tropical grassland with only a few trees. Savannas are clustered around the equator.

89. C: In the plate movement known as subduction, an oceanic plate slides underneath a continental plate. Oceanic plates are denser, so they tend to go beneath when they are pressed against lighter continental plates. The edge of the oceanic plate will be melted by the earth's mantle and may reemerge as a volcano. The Cascade Range of the northwest United States was formed by subduction. In faulting, the edges of two plates grind against each other laterally. The San Andreas Fault in California is perhaps the most famous example of this process. In spreading, plates pull apart from each other, typically creating a rift valley and the potential for earthquakes. In converging, two plates of similar density press against each other, creating mountain ranges where they meet.

90. A: There are tropical rain forests on all the continents except Europe and Antarctica. Indeed, the Congo River Basin in Africa is the site of the second-largest tropical rain forest. There are also tropical rain forests in Central America, northern Australia, and Southeast Asia. Of course, all these rain forests are close to the equator, where there is abundant heat and precipitation. All the other answer choices are true statements, though it could be said more specifically that tropical rain forests cover approximately 6 percent of the earth's surface.

91. A: Of the four answer choices, New York City is the most likely to be considered a modern cultural hearth. A cultural hearth is an area from which cultural trends emanate. Geographers suggest that there were seven original cultural hearths, including Mesoamerica and the Indus River Valley. The modes of living that originated in these areas emanated out into the rest of the world. These days, the cultural hearths tend to be the cities and countries with the most economic power. Of the four answer choices, New York City is clearly the wealthiest and the most influential. The styles and trends that originate in New York City find their way into communities all around the world.

92. B: Grinding wheat into flour is an example of secondary economic activity. A secondary economic activity is one in which raw materials are converted into a more valuable product. Another secondary economic activity would be weaving cotton into yarn. A primary economic activity is a direct use of natural resources. Hunting is one example of a primary economic activity. Service jobs are considered to be tertiary economic activities. These jobs do not necessarily entail the acquisition and use of raw materials. Lawyers and bus drivers are just two examples of tertiary economic actors. Quaternary economic activities entail the acquisition, synthesis, and production of information. Teachers and writers are among those who make up the quaternary level of economic activity.

93. C: In the United States, geographers typically define a hamlet as a settlement with fewer than 100 inhabitants. A hamlet may have a few businesses, but it is unlikely to have a post office or a government office. A village is slightly larger than a hamlet; it may contain about 500 to 1,000 people. A village is likely to have a grocery store. A town is larger than a village. It usually has about 2,500 inhabitants. A city is larger than a town.

94. D: When a person grows only enough food to feed himself and his family, he is engaged in subsistence farming. The peasants of undeveloped countries are often forced to rely on subsistence farming because they lack the equipment and water resources to expand their crop. Of course, subsistence farming is not an ideal arrangement because a drought or monsoon can wipe out an entire crop and endanger the lives of the farmers. Nomadic herding is constant migration accompanied by livestock, particularly cows or sheep. Commercial farming is large scale enough to allow some or all the crops to be sold in a market. Sharecropping is a system wherein a landowner allows tenant farmers to use his or her land in exchange for a portion of the harvest.

95. D: The popularity of hockey in Canada and the northern United States is an example of direct diffusion. Direct diffusion is the transfer of cultural practices and ideas between two groups living in close proximity to each other. Expansion diffusion, also known as forced diffusion, is the transfer of cultural practices from a subjugating culture to a subjugated culture. One example of expansion diffusion was the Western imposition of trading practices on China during the nineteenth and early twentieth centuries. Indirect diffusion is the spread of cultural traits over a long distance without there necessarily being any direct contact between the cultures. The popularity in the United States of henna tattoos, which originated in India, is an example of indirect diffusion.

96. D: More information is required to calculate the natural increase rate for Grassley County during this year. Natural increase rate is the growth in population measured as the surplus of live births over deaths for every thousand people. The calculation of natural increase rate does not take account of immigration or emigration. The natural increase rate for Grassley County cannot be calculated because the original population of the county is not given. As an example, if the beginning population of the county had been 10,000, the natural increase rate would be 40; $400 \times 1{,}000/10{,}000 = 40$.

97. C: Animistic religions include the belief that the natural world is imbued with spirits. Animists believe, for example, that trees, rocks, and animals are divine in some way. This sort of belief system is typical of Native Americans and the indigenous peoples of West Africa (for instance, the Asante). Many sociologists have noted that animist cultures often demonstrate greater reverence for the natural world. Monotheism is a belief that there is only one God. Christianity, Judaism, and Islam are all monotheistic religions. Pantheism is the belief that everything is a manifestation of the Divine Spirit. Polytheism is a belief in multiple gods. Hinduism is the most popular polytheistic religion.

98. B: Elections are not necessary to be recognized as a nation. Indeed, many nations are ruled by individuals or cabals who never allow elections to be held. Geographers assert that there are four criteria for nationhood: defined territory, government, sovereignty, and population. A nation must have land and other natural resources to exist. A nation also must have some form of government, whether it be tyrannical or democratic. Some level of central administration indicates the unity of the nation. A nation must have sovereignty; that is, it must not be directly controlled by some other country. Finally, and perhaps most obviously, a nation must have a population.

99. B: A sphere of influence is a region in which a foreign power has some political and economic control but does not directly govern. One classic example is the sphere of influence held by European nations in China in the nineteenth and early twentieth centuries. These regions were ostensibly still part of China but had their politics and trade manipulated by the governments of foreign nations. Spheres of influence are less formal than colonies or settlements, which are directly under the control of the foreign government. An enclave, meanwhile, is a country that is entirely surrounded by some other country.

100. C: Yemen is not a member of OPEC, the Organization of Petroleum Exporting Countries. Yemen has some deposits of oil, but the nation has only recently begun developing them. This, along with a desperate water shortage, accounts for Yemen's position as the poorest nation in the Middle East. OPEC was established in 1960 to set oil prices and production. Until the formation of OPEC, many oil-producing nations felt they were being exploited by Western oil companies. This organization has obtained a great deal of power and is held responsible for the gas shortages that wracked the United States during the late 1970s.

101. D: It is true that scarcity causes producers (and other people) to make choices. Producers must choose what to produce with limited resources. It is also true that the choices a producer makes when faced with scarcity come with trade-offs. There are advantages and disadvantages to different production decisions. And, finally, calculating the opportunity cost of a choice provides a manner with which to measure the consequence of a choice and compare that against the consequence of other choices.

102. D: Opportunity cost is a measure of what a society gives up to produce a good (or goods). When the society decides to increase its production of Good X from 10 to 15 units, it gives up the ability to produce 4 units of Good Y (with production of Good Y dropping from 10 units to 6 units). The opportunity cost of the decision, then, is 4 units of Good Y.

103. C: In the short-run Phillips curve, there is a trade-off between unemployment and inflation. There is no such trade-off in the long-run Phillips curve. According to the long-run Phillips curve, the economy tends to stay at the natural rate of unemployment, and any changes are minor variations that will self-correct.

104. C: When a nation follows the theory of comparative advantage, it specializes in producing the goods and services it can make at a lower opportunity cost and then engages in trade to obtain other goods.

105. A: As people have more and more of something, they value it less and less. This is the law of diminishing marginal utility, and it is what causes the downward slope of the demand curve.

106. B: The multiplier effect states that a given increase in spending, when multiplied by the multiplier, will lead to a given increase in AD. In this case, the \$1,000,000 spending increase and the multiplier of 5 lead to an AD increase of \$5,000,000 ($\$1,000,000 \times 5 = \$5,000,000$).

107. C: Answers A, B, and D are all correct. However, if the government imposes a tax on a good with a highly inelastic demand, producers can shift a lot of the cost of the tax onto consumers, since demand does not vary much as price increases.

108. C: The increased cost of gasoline increases the cost of transportation. This is a variable cost of supply, and so the aggregate supply curve shifts inward and upward. In the short run, aggregate demand would remain fixed, leading to a rise in prices and decreased GDP.

109. D: Firms in a monopolistic competition are not efficient. They earn a profit above the minimum ATC, meaning they are not efficient productively, and they create output at a level less than the level of allocative efficiency.

110. A: The Consumer Price Index is the value of a "market basket" of goods and services in one year compared to the value of the same goods and services in another year.

111. D: In the long run, aggregate supply does not depend on price. Aggregate supply in the long run depends strictly on the amount of capital and labor and the type of available technology.

112. A: The Phillips Curve says that inflation and unemployment have an indirect relationship. If the Fed acts to stop inflation, then according to the Phillips Curve, unemployment will increase.

113. C: A person who has taken out a fixed-rate loan can benefit from inflation by paying back the loan with dollars that are less valuable than they were when the loan was taken out. In the other examples, inflation harms the individual or entity.

114. D: Monetary policy is the practice of shrinking and growing the money supply in order to combat inflation and/or deflation and otherwise attempt to "adjust" the economy.

115. C: When the government increases taxes on corporations, it lowers their willingness to invest—represented by the Id curve. That means that the Id_{m1} curve will move to Id_{m2}, with a new equilibrium of C.

116. A: The nominal interest rate is stated interest rate, while the real interest rate is the nominal interest rate adjusted for inflation. If prices decrease during the period of the loan, the real interest rate will be less than the nominal interest rate.

117. B: The current account is part of what makes up a country's balance of payment account. The current account records the value of exports and imports of goods and services by a country, the country's net investment income, and the country's net transfers.

118. B: If interest rates in the US increase, foreign investors may send more money to the US. Those investors would have to first exchange their currencies for American dollars, making the American dollars more valued (scarce) and therefore increase in value.

119. B: Nominal GDP is the total dollar value of goods and services produced in a country in a year. However, since prices increase with inflation, nominal GDP gives a skewed view of an economy when looking at various years over time. Therefore, economists multiply nominal GDP by a price deflator that accounts for inflation in order to arrive at real GDP.

120. D: Culture can best be defined as the sum of everything that is learned by participating in a society. Choice A is incorrect because it is the specific definition of real culture, rather than a general definition of culture itself. Choice B defines ideal culture; again, this is a specific definition of a type of culture, rather than a definition of culture itself. Choice C refers not to culture, but to a cultural universal.

121. A: A major characteristic of ethnocentrism is the conviction that one's personal culture is the superior one.

122. D: A status set accurately defines multiple roles of the man described. Ascribed status (A), master status (B), and achieved status (C) all describe single, rather than multiple, roles which a man might assume.

123. A: The best characterization of sociocultural evolution is that it describes the inclination of organizations to increase in complexity in the long run. Choice B is incorrect because it is the description of society, not of sociocultural evolution. Choice C and Choice D are also wrong because they describe the ecological approach, not sociocultural evolution.

124. B: Randall Collins is the sociologist who defines modern conflict theory according to educational credentials. Karl Marx (A), Ralf Dahrendorf (C), and Max Weber (D) do not subscribe to this theory.

125. A: If an adult shoots a thief and others fire their own shots shortly thereafter, this is an illustration of the emergent-norm theory in action.

126. A: Behavioral neuroscience is the study of how the different parts of the body interact with one another and how this communication affects behavior. It deals mostly with the nervous system, which consists of brain structures, neurotransmitters, and neurons that are organized in a way that creates a pathway for information to move freely from one part of the body to another.

127. A: Basically, conditions of worth are an imposition by parents and others put on children to do what the parents or others want in order to be valued. This causes the child to give up her true self in order to please the person imposing these conditions of worth.

128. B: The learning or behavioral approach suggests that abnormal behavior is a learned behavior that has been classically or operantly conditioned in some way. Jesse's example shows how someone can teach a person how to behave abnormally. Jesse was operantly conditioned by his mother, who was only trying to help him. She did not understand that she was reinforcing abnormal behavior by rewarding him.

129. D: Stanley Milgram was responsible for doing a learning study in which teachers were told to shock students every time a wrong answer was given. The teachers were told that each shock would be progressively worse. If a teacher tried to decline participation, the authority would insist that the teacher continue. Even though electrical shocks were not being actually given, the teachers believed that the shocks were real. Students began to complain of physical symptoms as the supposed shocks increased. Sixty-three percent of the teachers delivered shocks until the end. This experiment was done to show the level of obedience to authority.

130. B: The Kitty Genovese incident actually happened in Queens, New York. The more witnesses there are, the less likely it is that someone will call for help in situations like this one, due to diffusion of responsibility. This diffusion leads to what is called the bystander effect.

Practice Test #2

1. Of the following European diseases that decimated the Inca population, which epidemic occurred the chronologically latest?

a. Typhus
b. Smallpox
c. Measles
d. Diphtheria

2. Which statement best describes the significance of the Mayflower Compact on colonial America?

a. It declared that the colonists were independent from King James.
b. It served as a blueprint for the later Bill of Rights.
c. It provided the Pilgrims the first written basis for laws in the New World.
d. It established Puritanism as the official religion for Puritan colonies.

3. European colonization of present-day Pennsylvania in the late 17th century is most closely associated with:

a. The desire for freedom of the press
b. Escape from high taxes
c. The desire for religious freedom
d. Escape from trade restrictions

4. Which statement best describes the significance of the Peter Zenger trial in colonial America?

a. It was the earliest American case on the right to bear arms.
b. It established a precedent for freedom of the press.
c. It was the earliest American case on right of peaceable assembly.
d. It established a precedent for freedom of religion.

5. Some American colonists reacted angrily to Great Britain's Navigation Acts in the seventeenth and eighteenth centuries primarily because of which of the following?

a. The Acts restricted manufacturing in the colonies.
b. The Acts forced the colonists to buy sugar from the French West Indies.
c. The Acts gave the British a monopoly on tobacco.
d. The Acts placed high taxes on the cost of shipping goods to Britain.

6. The French and Indian War ended in 1763. Which subsequent British policy regarding the American colonies was most important to the American Revolution?

a. Increasingly limited oversight of the colonies in order to focus on Canadian territories
b. A determination that the colonies should help pay for the War
c. The Proclamation of 1763 limiting the location of new American colonies
d. Increasing the colonies' dependence on the British military

7. Which of the following is the most significant justification for United States expansion as advocated by the Manifest Destiny?

a. It was the duty of the United States to spread democracy.
b. The United States would spread material wealth.
c. It was the duty of the United States to prevent the spread of slavery.
d. The United States would spread religious freedom.

8. The Treaty of Guadalupe Hidalgo ended the war between the United States and Mexico. The treaty ceded which of the following present-day states to the US?

a. California, New Mexico, Wyoming, and parts of Utah
b. California, New Mexico, and parts of Colorado, Nevada, and Ohio
c. California, Nevada, Utah, New Mexico, and parts of Arizona, Colorado, Oklahoma, Kansas and Wyoming
d. California, New Mexico, and parts of Arizona and Utah

9. Which statement best describes the significance of the Battle of Chapultepec during the US-Mexican War?

a. General Zachary Taylor's performance gained him recognition as an American hero.
b. It was the first Mexican victory after a long string of Mexican defeats.
c. General Santa Ana narrowly escaped capture during the battle.
d. It was the last major US assault prior to capturing Mexico City.

10. During the Civil War, General William T. Sherman led Union troops in a march from Atlanta to Savannah. Which is the best description of the goal of this March to the Sea?

a. Preventing Confederate access to Savannah
b. Distracting Robert E. Lee's troops from their engagement in Maryland
c. Breaking the will to fight among Southern civilians as well as soldiers
d. Freeing slaves who might otherwise contribute to the Confederate cause

11. After the Civil War, President Andrew Johnson disagreed with Congress over Reconstruction policies. Which action by President Johnson best describes the grounds for which he was impeached?

a. He dismissed a Cabinet member without congressional permission.
b. He refused to enforce the Fourteenth Amendment.
c. He sought to disenfranchise former Confederate officers.
d. He violated Constitution law in forming a third political party.

12. Which statement best describes how the Spanish-American War in 1898 shaped the international standing of the United States?

a. The United States gained new international respect through the strategic brilliance and efficiency of the US Army.
b. The US weakened its moral authority by being the first nation in the conflict to declare war.
c. The sinking of the US Battleship Maine cast international doubts on the power of the US Navy.
d. The United States gained new international power by acquiring Guam, Puerto Rico, and the Philippines.

13. Which of the following is the most accurate description of the relationship between agriculture and industry in the 19th century?

a. With industrial and technological advances, farming was left behind in favor of industrial work.
b. With more urban workers needing food, farming became more important than industrial work.
c. Specialization and mechanization were applied more to agriculture at this time than to industry.
d. The development of both agriculture and industry was helped by technological innovations.

14. The Populist Party most contributed to the prominence of which issue in the United States in the late 19th and early 20th centuries?

a. The rising cost of farm crops
b. The justification for the Electoral College
c. The basis for US currency
d. The rights of organized labor

15. The United States fought North Vietnam in the 1960s and 1970s primarily to:

a. Spread democracy modeled on the US system
b. Demonstrate US power to the Soviet Union
c. Protect US trade interests in Southeast Asia
d. Prevent the spread of communism

16. How did isolationism most influence American society in the decade following World War I?

a. It shaped a temporarily strong economy as the US avoided the troubled economies of postwar Europe.
b. It led to a system of admitting immigrants according to quotas based on their national origins.
c. It guided the US government's decision to strengthen its navy as a safeguard against foreign attacks.
d. It influenced the collapse of trade deals, allowing US companies access to oil in Colombia and in Middle Eastern countries.

17. Which of the following best describes the main idea of the passage?

The US decision to drop the atomic bomb on Japan during World War II is a complex one that has received little examination by most ordinary American citizens. Many citizens are under the impression that the decision to use the bomb on Japan was primarily based on a desire to prevent a bloody and prolonged war on Japanese soil, with the view that the use of the bomb thus saved many more American lives – perhaps many more American and Japanese lives – that would otherwise have been lost.

Much less considered, however, is the fact that prior to the bombing of Hiroshima and Nagasaki, the United States government believed not only that Japan was losing the war, but that Japan was considering how best to surrender. Note: Japan was considering not whether to surrender, but under what conditions Japan could surrender. Viewed in this light, the US decision to drop the bomb seems to have rather less to do with bringing a swift end to World War II than with the looming Cold War: in dropping the bomb, the United States demonstrated its power to the Soviet Union and its willingness to use that power. This casts a rather different perspective on the bombing, a perspective we would do well to consider in this age of terrorist threats and weapons of mass destruction. Under what circumstances is the use of such deadly weapons on civilians justified?

a. The justification for the bombing of Japan in WWII is a highly nuanced topic that many Americans have likely not considered at great depth.
b. The use of weapons of mass destruction on civilians is not justified.
c. Many Americans are mistaken about why the United States uses deadly weapons.
d. The United States used the atomic bomb on an enemy that was already defeated.

18. United States Secretary of State Henry Kissinger most influenced the course of the Cold War by:

a. Helping to slow the United States-Soviet Union arms race
b. Helping to establish a cease-fire in the Arab-Israeli War in 1973
c. Leaving the Soviet Union out of US efforts to end the Vietnam War
d. Ordering a bombing campaign in Laos and Cambodia

19. During the Cuban Missile Crisis, what did Soviet President Nikita Khrushchev demand in exchange for the removal of Soviet missile launching sites from Cuba?

a. A guarantee that the United States would not invade Cuba
b. The removal of US missile launching sites from an island off the Soviet coast
c. An apology for the US naval blockade that prevented Soviet access to Cuba
d. Negotiations regarding the production of nuclear weapons

20. Which statement best describes how the 1944 passage of the G.I. Bill most influenced US society?

a. It dramatically increased retention in the US military.
b. It offered limited free housing for veterans.
c. It helped create a new middle class in US society.
d. It transformed the work force by privileging veterans.

21. Which is the best description of how Jonas Salk's 1955 development of the polio vaccine most affected American society?

a. The invention drastically reduced the incidence of polio in the United States.
b. The vaccine caused polio in some people who received the vaccine.
c. The announcement of the vaccine sparked a debate regarding the media and science.
d. The vaccine ignited a vigorous search for a cancer vaccine.

22. Under President Franklin Roosevelt, New Deal legislation sought to restore faith in the banking system by:

a. Creating a Public Works Administration to oversee banking institutions
b. Requiring banks to loan money at certain interest rates
c. Shifting ownership of prominent banks to the federal government
d. Establishing a corporation to insure bank deposits

23. The "sit-ins" of the civil rights movement during the 1960s were most important to which subsequent reform?

a. Integration of the United States armed forces
b. Banning of literacy tests as a requirement for voter registration
c. Integration of lunch counters, theaters, and other businesses
d. The Supreme Court decision outlawing "separate but equal" schools

24. Martin Luther King, Jr. and Malcolm X were both important figures in the American civil rights movement. Which of the following statements best describes a difference between their respective approaches to civil rights?

a. Martin Luther King, Jr. advocated nonviolence; Malcolm X advocated self-defense against white aggression.
b. Martin Luther King, Jr. mobilized ordinary citizens; Malcolm X focused on working with local white political leaders.
c. Martin Luther King, Jr. related Christianity to civil rights; Malcolm X did not link religion to civil rights.
d. Martin Luther King, Jr. promoted Black Nationalism; Malcolm X did not.

25. In 1973, the US Congress passed the War Powers Act. How did the Act reassert congressional authority relative to that of the President?

a. It mandated congressional approval for funding war-related expenses.
b. It required the President to submit regular reports to Congress regarding conflicts lasting more than 60 days.
c. It restricted the power of the President to suspend key elements of the Constitution.
d. It limited the length of time the President can dispatch combat troops without congressional approval.

26. Of the following landmark US Supreme Court decisions, which one addressed the regulation of interstate navigation?

a. *Gibbons v. Ogden* (1824)
b. *Ableman v. Booth* (1859)
c. *Plessy v. Ferguson* (1896)
d. *The Paquete Habana* (1900)

27. Which of the following statements is NOT correct concerning feminism in the 1970s and 1980s?

a. President Ronald Reagan appointed Sandra Day O'Connor as the first female Supreme Court justice.
b. The administration of Republican President Ronald Reagan was generally against feminist goals.
c. The Equal Rights Amendment, which supported the goals of feminism, was passed by Congress in 1972.
d. The Equal Rights Amendment was ratified by Congress in 1983.

28. How did Egypt's geographical features most contribute to the stability of ancient Egyptian civilization?

a. The Nile River regularly and predictably flooded, irrigating crops.
b. The expanse of the Nile River prevented Egyptians from settling elsewhere.
c. The Valley of the Kings divided Upper Egypt from Lower Egypt.
d. The Mediterranean Sea enabled contact between Egyptians and other ancient peoples.

29. How does the prevalence of ziggurats in ancient Mesopotamia illustrate a central factor of Mesopotamian culture?

a. Intended as lookouts, the number of ziggurats illustrates a Mesopotamian concern for security from invaders.
b. Used for stargazing, the number of ziggurats shows how Mesopotamian culture depended on astrology.
c. Dedicated to Mesopotamian rulers, the ziggurats illustrate the complete control Mesopotamian kings held over their subjects.
d. Structures dedicated to gods, the ziggurats illustrate the importance of religion in Mesopotamian culture.

30. Arabic mathematics most contributed to the development of mathematics in the Western world by:

a. Founding the mathematics of calculus
b. Using negative numbers in mathematical equations
c. Founding the mathematics of probability
d. Making important advances in algebra

31. Which of the following statements is NOT true of Minoan culture?

a. The name honors King Minos.
b. Its capital was in Knossos on the island of Crete.
c. Minoan culture was overtaken by the Athenians.
d. Its capital was a maze-like structure of many chambers.

32. The word democracy comes from two Greek root words meaning what?

a. People and rule
b. People and vote
c. City and state
d. Tyrant and overthrow

33. Of the following cultural developments influenced by the Catholic Church, which did NOT occur before the 15th century AD?

a. Romanesque architecture
b. Gothic architectural style
c. Baroque arts, Jesuit order
d. Renaissance works of art

34. How did Charlemagne's coronation as Holy Roman Emperor influence European politics?

a. It united much of Western Europe under a single ruler.
b. It strengthened papal authority regarding the right of political leaders to rule.
c. It made Catholicism the official religion throughout Charlemagne's empire.
d. It led to Charlemagne's renunciation of conquest by force.

35. Which statement best describes the feudal society of Western Europe in the Middle Ages?

a. Religious institutions owned most of the land and leased portions to vassals.
b. Rulers granted land strictly on the basis of blood relationships.
c. Rulers granted vassals land in exchange for military and political service.
d. Feudalism shifted a spice-based economy to a land-based economy.

36. Which of the following played the most influential role in the Spanish defeat of the Incas in the 16th century?

a. The scarcity of roads in the Incan Empire prevented the Incas from easily defending their cities.
b. Francisco Pizarro's forces outnumbered the Incan warriors.
c. The centralized power structure of the Incan Empire left the Incas vulnerable after Atahualpa was captured.
d. New diseases introduced by the Spanish decimated the Incan army.

37. In about 1428, the Mesoamerican city-states Tenochtitlan, Texcoco, and Tlacopan formed a Triple Alliance. How did this influence Aztec history?

a. Texcoco and Tlacopan secretly conspired against Tenochtitlan, using the Alliance as a front.
b. Disagreements about strategy between the city-states weakened Aztec resistance to Spanish invaders.
c. The alliance agreed that each city-state would offer a specific number of human sacrifices each year.
d. The allied city-states joined forces to conquer other city-states, incorporating them into an Aztec Empire.

38. In the 16th century, Akbar ruled the Mughal Empire, which covered much of present-day India. Which statement best describes one means by which Akbar maintained control of the Empire?

a. He paid administrative officials with land instead of money.
b. He accommodated the religious practices of Hindus as well as Muslims.
c. He refused to allow certain defeated rulers to keep their land.
d. He refused to allow the construction of Hindu temples.

39. Which statement best describes the role played by the French economy in causing the 1789 French Revolution?

a. France's very large national debt led to heavy tax burdens on the French peasantry.
b. Nearly seventy percent of annual national expenditures financed luxuries for the French nobility.
c. Reforms in the guild system allowed many peasants to rise to the middle class.
d. The king's attempt to curtail free trade led skilled journeymen to rebel against the monarchy.

40. A French peasant girl, Joan of Arc, had visions from the saints. What did they tell her to do?

a. Lead French troops to attack the English.
b. Lead troops to retake control of Jerusalem.
c. Become the first female priest in the Catholic Church.
d. Overthrow Charles VII of France.

41. How did Russia's participation in World War I influence the Russian Revolution?

a. Civilian suffering and military setbacks served as a catalyst for revolutionary forces.
b. Nicholas III capitalized on battlefield successes to temporarily silence critics.
c. The government eased laws banning collective action by factory workers to appease social discontent about the war.
d. Anti-government protesters temporarily ceased protesting to show patriotism in a difficult war.

42. How did World War II influence American society?

a. Consumption decreased in postwar American society.
b. Thousands of people moved to find work in war-related factories.
c. Racially integrated army units helped desegregate American society.
d. Japanese-Americans were banned from serving in the US military.

43. How did the Truman Doctrine shape US foreign policy after World War II?

a. It influenced President Truman's decision to create commissions on civil rights.
b. It shaped the US role in rebuilding the economies of postwar Europe.
c. It led the US government to refrain from interfering with the US economy.
d. It led to US military involvement in countries such as Korea.

44. Which one of these landmark Supreme Court decisions involving the right to an attorney took place sometime after the Cold War?

a. *Gideon v. Wainwright*
b. *Montejo v. Louisiana*
c. *Escobedo v. Illinois*
d. *Miranda v. Arizona*

45. During the 15th century, Johann Gutenberg invented a printing press with moveable type. How did his invention influence science?

a. It did not influence science; the printing of Gutenberg Bibles directed public attention away from science and toward reforming the Catholic Church.
b. It led to scientific advances throughout Europe by spreading scientific knowledge.
c. It influenced scientific advancement in Germany only, where Gutenberg's press was based.
d. It did not influence science; though texts with scientific knowledge were printed, distribution of these texts was limited.

46. How did Plato's Theory of Forms most influence Christianity?

a. It held that what is most real and most good is outside the physical realm.
b. The theory described a cosmic conflict between ideal forms of good and evil.
c. It held that the form of the good formed a trinity with ideal forms of knowledge and reason.
d. The theory described Socratic reasoning as a means of redemption from sin.

47. Which statement best describes the role of the Catholic Church in medieval Western Europe?

a. Powerful and wealthy, the Church was important to both poor and rich people.
b. The Church concerned itself mainly with the poorer members of medieval society.
c. Weakened by infighting about Church doctrine, the Church struggled to wield power.
d. The Catholic Church served as a neutral force between competing political leaders.

48. What effect did the Crusades have on Europe's Jewish population?

a. Entire European Jewish communities were killed during the First Crusade.
b. Persecution of Jewish people declined as the Crusaders focused on Muslims.
c. Most Jewish traders and merchants profited through Crusades-related business.
d. To avoid persecution, some Jewish-only battalions fought in each Crusade.

49. Which statement best describes how Martin Luther's religious Reformation influenced Western civilization?

a. It contributed to the decline of women's and girls' education.
b. It weakened civil authorities in European towns.
c. It contributed to the rise of individualism.
d. It delayed reform within the Catholic Church itself.

50. Which factor of the Neolithic Revolution most directly contributed to the practice of trade?

a. More freedom for people to choose where they lived
b. The rise of new religious practices
c. The ability of communities to stockpile surplus food
d. New advances in tools

51. Which of the following statements best describes how Cubism reflected a changing world in the early 20th century?

a. It depicted subjects from multiple perspectives.
b. It portrayed the human body as sacrosanct.
c. It eschewed rationality in favor of emotion.
d. It used unusually vivid colors and color schemes.

52. Which of the following resources in the West Bank is the most significant motivation for Israel's continuing occupation of that territory?

a. The Mediterranean Sea
b. Oil reserves
c. Olive groves
d. Aquifers

53. The link between female activists and the temperance movement in the 19th century is best explained by concerns regarding the relationship between alcohol and:

a. Racial violence
b. Lost productivity
c. Domestic violence
d. Infertility

54. Which of the following is NOT true regarding the Whiskey Rebellion?

a. Washington's dispatching federal troops did not resolve the revolt, a setback for the government.
b. An excise tax levied on whiskey was central to Treasury Secretary Hamilton's revenue program.
c. Farmers in Pennsylvania objected to the excise tax on whiskey, and were refusing to pay the tax.
d. Farmers in Pennsylvania committed acts of terrorism against tax collectors over the whiskey tax.

55. Which of the following statements does NOT describe Rome's relationship with its conquered peoples?

a. All subjects were granted the full range of rights entitled to Roman citizens.
b. The Romans allowed some degree of cultural autonomy.
c. Subjects were expected to follow Roman laws.
d. Subjects were obligated to pay taxes.

56. Civic responsibility differs from personal responsibility in that the subject matter of civic responsibility is mainly which of the following?

a. Fair reporting of government actions
b. Fair dealings between governments
c. A person's responsibilities as a citizen
d. A person's responsibilities as a government worker

57. Social studies education has many practical applications. Which of the following is the most direct application of teaching high school seniors the structure of the US government?

a. Knowledge of the fundamentals of federalism
b. Informed participation in school elections
c. Knowledge of a system of checks and balances
d. Informed participation in US political processes

58. Thomas Paine's *Common Sense* influenced which American document that ultimately helped shape the Constitution?

a. The Articles of Confederation
b. The Declaration of Independence
c. The Bill of Rights
d. The Treaty of Greenville

59. The concept of due process in the Fifth Amendment to the U.S. Constitution protects individuals in which of the following ways?

a. Guaranteeing a citizen's right to a trial by jury within a reasonable timeframe
b. Restricting the government's ability to remove basic rights without following the law
c. Guaranteeing a citizen's right to equal protection under the law
d. Restricting the government's ability to remove basic rights without dire cause

60. Which court case established the Court's ability to overturn laws that violated the Constitution?

a. *Miranda v. Arizona*
b. *Marbury v. Madison*
c. *United States v. Curtiss-Wright Export Corporation*
d. *Brown v. Board of Education of Topeka*

61. The US government is best understood as a federalist government because:

a. The legislative branch consists of two representative bodies.
b. It is a representative democracy rather than a direct democracy.
c. Political power is divided between the federal government and the states.
d. A national Constitution shapes national legislation.

62. In 1777, the United States Congress adopted the Articles of Confederation. The Articles of Confederation limited the power of the federal government by denying it:

a. The power to borrow money
b. The power to declare war
c. The power to make international treaties
d. The power to raise taxes

63. The Seventeenth Amendment to the US Constitution made the US government more democratic in which of the following ways?

a. By requiring state governors to be selected by popular election rather than by state electoral colleges
b. By mandating a regular national census to reevaluate state representation in the House of Representatives
c. By requiring US senators to be selected by popular election rather than by state legislatures
d. By mandating regular state censuses to determine appropriate representation in state Houses of Representatives

64. Which line of the chart below best lists the kinds of cases over which the US federal court system has jurisdiction?

Jurisdiction of the Federal Court System

Line 1	Constitutional law	Bankruptcy	Most contract cases
Line 2	Constitutional law	Most contract cases	Most criminal cases
Line 3	Constitutional law	Bankruptcy	Disputes between states
Line 4	Constitutional law	Most personal injury cases	Disputes between states

a. Line 1
b. Line 2
c. Line 3
d. Line 4

65. Which branch(es) of the federal government issue(s) subpoenas?

I. The executive branch
II. The legislative branch
III. The judicial branch

a. III only
b. I and III
c. II and III
d. II only

66. Which statement best describes how the 1896 US Supreme Court decision in *Plessy v. Ferguson* most influenced US society?

a. It reinforced the rights of individual states.
b. It legalized poll taxes and similar measures.
c. It provided a legal basis for racial segregation.
d. It determined the legality of railway strikes.

67. Which is true of the President's authority?

a. The President has the authority to declare war.
b. The President has the authority to grant pardons and clemencies for federal crimes, except in cases of impeachment.
c. The President can serve three terms.
d. The President has the authority to appoint the Speaker of the House.

68. In the United States, the Electoral College elects the President and Vice President. How many Electoral College members are allowed to each state?

a. The state's number of US Representatives plus counties
b. The state's number of US Senators plus Representatives
c. The state's number of US Representatives plus state Secretaries
d. The state's number of US Senators plus counties

Refer to the following for questions 69–70:

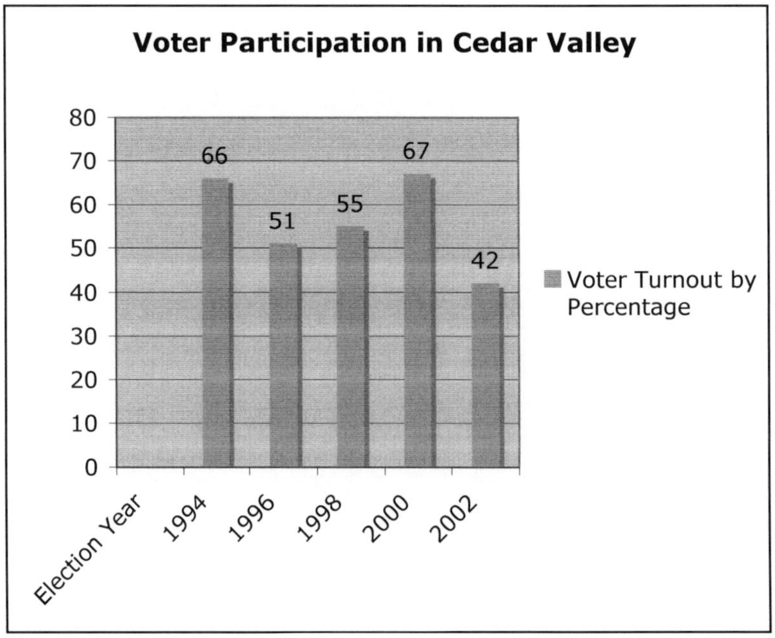

69. Applying generally-accepted principles of statistical analysis, what is the range of data for voter participation?

a. 55
b. 0-80
c. 25
d. 42-67

70. What is the median for voter participation?

a. 56.2%
b. 55%
c. 50%
d. 40%

71. One of the earliest political parties in the United States was the Federalist Party. Its decline is best explained by:

a. A failure to organize state political parties
b. The enmity of wealthy Americans
c. Its opposition to the War of 1812
d. Its advocacy of a strong central government

72. Which of the following is a significant structural similarity between the government of the Iroquois Confederacy and the government of the United States?

a. Many decisions require compromise between two separate entities. In the Iroquois Confederacy, those entities were two different sets of Lords; in the US government, those entities are the House of Representatives and the Senate.
b. A single leader has significant executive powers: in the Iroquois Confederacy, a chief, and in the US government, the president.
c. The level of representation in at least one legislative body depended on population. In the Iroquois Confederacy, the population of tribes partially determined representation, and in the United States, the population of states partially determines representation.
d. A third judicial branch served as a check on the executive power in both the Iroquois Confederacy and the US government.

73. Which statement best describes the significance of Hammurabi's Code?

a. It restructured Babylonian society.
b. It helped establish a precedent for codifying law.
c. It established the same penalties for all law-breakers.
d. It instituted penalties mainly in terms of fines.

74. A historical antecedent of democracy is the government of ancient Athens. Which statement best describes a central feature of Athenian democracy?

a. Athenians practiced direct democracy, not representative democracy.
b. The right to vote depended on the wealth of a person's family.
c. Campaigns for political office traditionally involved religious leaders.
d. The right to vote could not be stripped from a citizen.

75. Cases involving diplomats and ambassadors fall under the jurisdiction of which court?

a. District courts
b. State courts
c. Supreme Court
d. Federal Court of Appeals

76. What portion of the federal budget is dedicated to transportation, education, national resources, the environment, and international affairs?

a. Mandatory spending
b. Discretionary spending
c. Undistributed offsetting receipts
d. Official budget outlays

77. What is one reason for using a secondary source over a primary source?

a. To understand an event through a first-hand account
b. Primary sources are text-only
c. To understand an event through accounts after the fact
d. Primary sources are only visual

Refer to the following for questions 78–79:

> I was very young, but I remember sitting in our living room watching the television the day of the first moon landing, in 1969. It was a black and white television—my family didn't have a color one till later—and we all gathered in the room and watched the pictures. I'm not sure how they got the pictures to us, but I think it involved satellites around the earth they'd made especially for that purpose. The satellites captured the pictures and somehow beamed them into our televisions, live. That just showed again how our technology, American technology, had become much more advanced than Russian technology. The moon was pocked and pitted, like a big pumice stone. Watching Neil Armstrong walk on the moon was like nothing I'd ever imagined, and because of that somehow it was less surprising; I'd never thought it was impossible. Afterwards I went outside with my parents and my brother and we just kind of stared at the moon and imagined that people were on it, all those miles away.

78. For which of the following lesson units would this primary source be most appropriate?

a. Having students learn what it was like to witness the first moon landing
b. Teaching students about the surface of the moon
c. Teaching about the technology used to show the moon landing live on television
d. Having students learn about changes in television use

79. Which of the following claims by the author is the claim most likely to be influenced by bias?

a. The first moon landing occurred in 1969.
b. The author's family watched the moon landing on a black and white TV.
c. Satellites captured the live images from the moon landing.
d. American technology was much more advanced than Russian technology.

80. A typical case study in the field of social studies primarily involves:

a. Gathering qualitative data
b. Gathering quantitative data
c. Statistical analysis
d. No researcher/subject contact

81. Suppose you are teaching a unit on different forms of government. Which of the following is the best way to teach students to write critically in relation to this topic?

a. Ask the students to write an essay regarding why one form of government is better than another.
b. Have the students give organized, written descriptions of the different characteristics of each form of government.
c. Ask the students to write a creative work from the point of view of someone living under one of the forms of government.
d. Have the students write a report on a country that uses a specific form of government.

82. Consider the map below. Shaded areas indicate water use, with darker areas indicating heavier use. On the basis of the map, which of the following is the best inference regarding the areas where there is no shading?

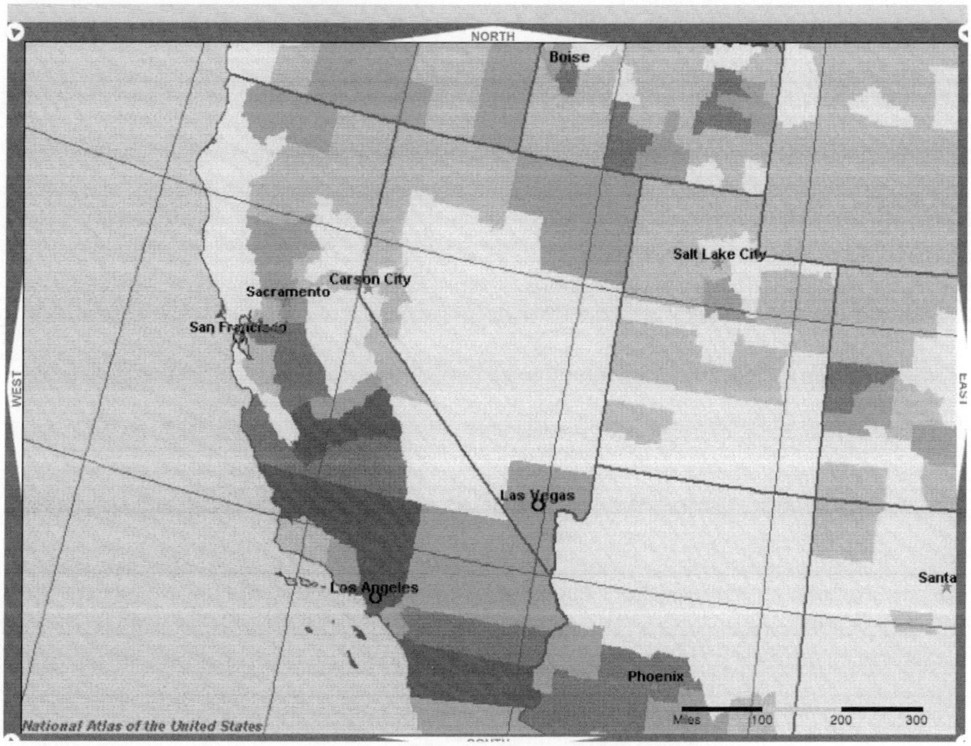

Map source: http://www.nationalatlas.gov/natlas/Natlasstart.asp

a. They are less inhabited.
b. They are more desert-like.
c. Residents are better at conservation.
d. Residents require less water per capita.

83. The apparent distance between Greenland and Norway is greatest on a(n)

a. Mercator Map
b. Conic Projection Map
c. Contour Map
d. Equal-Area Projection Map

84. Which of the following Roman numerals indicates the Colorado River in the figure below?

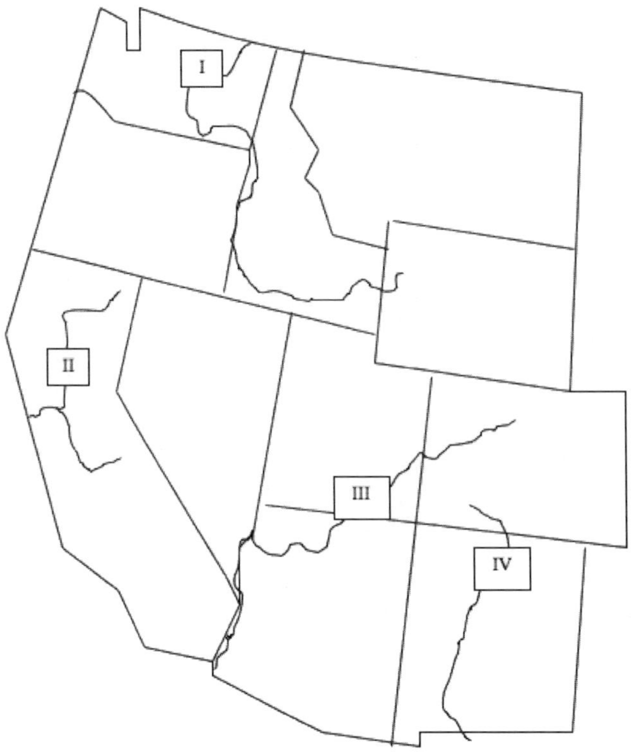

a. I
b. II
c. III
d. IV

85. On a globe, the distance between Buenos Aires and Tokyo is 35 cm. If the globe has a scale of 1 cm for every 516 km, what is the real distance?

a. 18,060 km
b. 35 km
c. 21,080 km
d. 14,740 km

86. Water is continuously recycled in the hydrosphere. By which process does water return to the atmosphere after precipitation?

a. Percolation
b. Cohesion
c. Evaporation
d. Condensation

87. When the Northern Hemisphere of the Earth experiences summer, the Southern Hemisphere experiences winter. This is best explained by:

a. The changing distance of the Earth from the sun
b. The angle of the Earth as it revolves around the sun
c. The changing speed of the Earth's orbit
d. The shape of the Earth relative to the sun

88. Which geographic features were most conducive to the development of early civilizations?

a. Rivers
b. Deserts
c. Forests
d. Mountains

89. In which environment would you most likely find animals that estivate, or sleep during the day?

a. Desert
b. Temperate forest
c. Tundra
d. Grasslands

90. World population growth has most significantly impacted which of the following aspects of Earth's physical environment?

a. Deforestation
b. Increased biodiversity
c. Shrinking ocean "dead zones"
d. Mass extinction events

91. What is the name of the highest habitable region in Middle and South America?

a. *Tierra fria*
b. *Puna*
c. *Tierra helada*
d. *Templada*

92. Which of the following countries has the least amount of arable land by percent of total landmass?

a. China
b. Italy
c. Germany
d. Japan

93. Why is Mecca an important site for Muslims?

a. It is the birthplace of the prophet Muhammad.
b. According to the Koran, the Second Coming will occur in Mecca.
c. Muhammad fled to Mecca from Medina in 622 AD.
d. It is home of the Ka'ba, a holy structure said to be built by Abraham.

94. What is the Noble Eightfold Path in Buddhism?

a. Samsara, the cycle of birth, death, and rebirth
b. Moral life as a means to end suffering
c. The Buddhist precepts of ethical conduct
d. The realization that self is an illusion

95. Stephen travels to the city every morning for work. Every evening, he returns to his home in the suburbs. What kind of movement is this?

a. Cyclic movement
b. Migratory movement
c. Cross-boundary movement
d. Periodic movement

96. Which of the following statements best describes one effect of opening the Suez Canal?

a. It led to further European involvement and colonization of Asia.
b. It provided a trade route between the Mediterranean and Black Seas.
c. It led to more peaceful relations in the Middle East.
d. It served as a strategic route for military forces.

97. Which of the following is NOT one of the world's four major population agglomerations?

a. North Africa
b. Eastern North America
c. South Asia
d. Europe

98. The town of Hamilton has 400 citizens living in 12 square miles. The town of Burrsville has 300 citizens living over 10 square miles. Which town has the greater population density?

a. Hamilton has the greater population density.
b. Burrsville has the greater population density.
c. The towns have the same population density.
d. The answer cannot be determined based on the information given.

99. Which of the following is NOT one of the demographic variables?

a. Fertility
b. Diversity
c. Mortality
d. Migration

100. What has been one result of NAFTA?

a. The border between the United States and Mexico has opened.
b. There has been significant migration from Canada to Mexico.
c. Trade barriers between the United States and Canada have increased.
d. Mexico has sought to enter other trade agreements.

101. An action's opportunity cost is best explained in terms of which of the following?

a. The minimum amount a business must borrow for the action
b. The opportunities given up in order to pursue that action
c. The percentage of one's overall budget that the action requires
d. The cost of a long-term action adjusted for inflation

102. The economic theories of John Maynard Keynes are most closely associated with which of the following?

a. The view that deficit spending leads to inflation
b. Advocating government action against monopolies
c. The view that supply creates its own demand
d. Advocating government action to stimulate economic growth

103. How did Eli Whitney's invention of the cotton gin in 1793 most influence the US economy?

a. It elevated cotton as a basis of the Southern economy.
b. It led to many smaller cotton plantations.
c. It reduced the need for the US to import cotton.
d. It decreased the dependence of plantations on slave labor.

104. Consider the graph below. Which of the following is true?

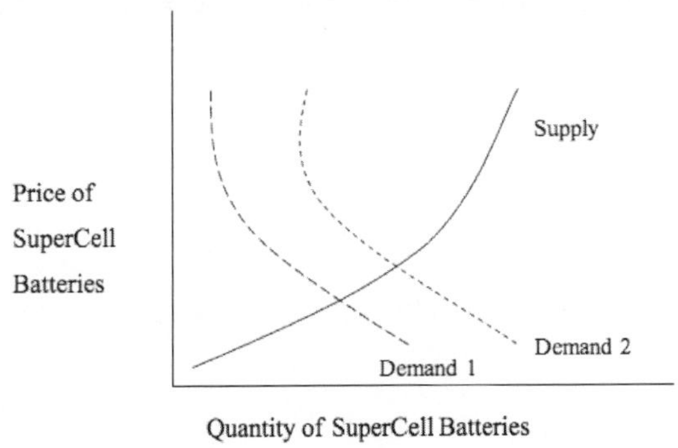

a. The price has decreased with a shift in supply.
b. The equilibrium point has remained constant.
c. The price has risen with a shift in demand.
d. There a double coincidence of wants.

105. Which of the following is the most effective use of technology for showing a class of students the relationship between supply and demand?

a. Asking the students to maintain a class wiki listing those and other key economic terms
b. Having students look up definitions of "supply" and "demand" in an online dictionary
c. Using presentation software to show students different supply and demand curves
d. Using spreadsheet software to track the rise and fall of demand of a given product

106. Which of the following assignments is the best means of assessing a student's ability to apply knowledge of the concepts of supply and demand?

a. Write detailed definitions of "supply" and "demand."
b. Write a detailed interpretation of a supply and demand curve.
c. Write a report on the history of a recession.
d. Write a compare/contrast essay on free-market systems versus others.

107. Which statement best describes the difference between a monopoly and an oligopoly?

a. A monopoly involves a single supplier of a good or service; an oligopoly involves a small number of suppliers of a good or service.
b. An oligopoly is a monopoly operating under price ceilings.
c. In a monopoly, one company owns a single plant that produces a given good; in an oligopoly, one company owns several plants that produce a given good.
d. An oligopoly is a legalized monopoly.

108. When should a firm shut down in the short run?

a. If total costs are greater than total revenues
b. If total variable costs are greater than total revenues
c. If total fixed costs are greater than total revenues
d. A and B

109. The US government seeks to reduce unemployment in part to prevent individuals from suffering hardship. How is unemployment also most likely to affect the economy in the short run?

a. By causing inflation
b. By leading to lost productivity
c. By increasing aggregate demand
d. By increasing aggregate supply

110. Which of the following is included in the unemployment rate typically followed by economists?

I. Structural unemployment
II. Frictional unemployment
III. Cyclical unemployment

a. I only
b. II only
c. III only
d. I and II only

111. Which combination of factors is most likely to cause inflation?

a. High unemployment and reduced production
b. Credit restrictions and reduced production
c. An oversupply of currency and a relatively low number of available goods
d. An undersupply of currency and a relatively low number of available goods

112. Which of the following curves represents the long-run Phillips curve?

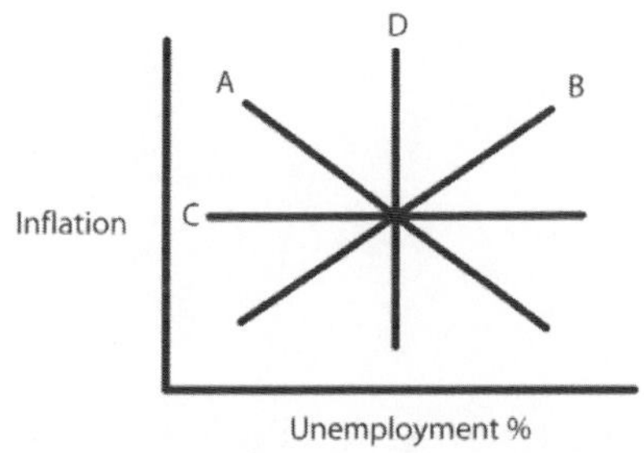

a. A
b. B
c. C
d. D

113. A business can be a corporation, partnership, or sole proprietorship. For a business owner, what is one advantage of running a corporation instead of a sole proprietorship?

a. Corporations offer limited liability protection.
b. Corporations avoid the "double tax" problem.
c. Corporations are more expensive to form.
d. Corporations are easier to dissolve.

114. In 1890, the US government passed the Sherman Antitrust Act. The Act has been most influential in restricting anticompetitive practices by:

a. Outlawing acts that restrained interstate trade
b. Its use in dissolving the Standard Oil trust
c. Outlawing acts that restrained intrastate trade
d. By its use in dissolving the AT&T monopoly

115. Sally's grandmother kept $100,000 in a cookie jar for years but recently gave it to Sally, who immediately puts it in her bank in a savings account. The bank has a 20% reserve rate. Which of the following is true?

I. Excess reserves increase by $20,000
II. The bank's money supply increases by as much as $120,000
III. There is no change in the bank's money supply

a. I only
b. I and II
c. III
d. None of the above

116. Which of the following is the most frequently used tool of the Federal Reserve to control monetary policy?

a. Changing the interest rate at which banks can borrow from the Federal Reserve
b. Buying and selling stock options to raise or reduce interest rates
c. Adjusting the percentage of deposits a bank is required to keep on hand
d. Buying and selling government bonds to raise or reduce interest rates

117. A country's currency increases in value on foreign currency exchange markets. What will happen as a result?

I. Exports will drop
II. Imports will rise
III. The balance of payments will rise

a. I only
b. II only
c. I and II
d. II and III

118. Assume that the exchange rate between US dollars and Canadian dollars floats freely, and that American demand for Canadian dollars decreases. What is likely to happen?

a. Imports of American goods into Canada will increase.
b. The price of Canadian dollars in terms of American dollars will increase.
c. The price of US goods in Canadian dollars will decrease.
d. The price of Canadian goods in American dollars will decrease.

119. Which of the following could best be used in order to determine the "price deflator" for converting nominal GDP to real GDP?

a. Consumer Price Index
b. Gross National Product
c. Business Cycle
d. Phillips Curve

120. A founder of modern psychology, Wilhelm Wundt studied the components of experience. Many philosophers had also done so. Which statement best describes why Wundt's studies helped found the specific study of psychology?

a. He collected data in an attempt to test his views.
b. He sought to explain experience in terms of publicly-observable behavior.
c. His written works outlined a single sophisticated theory of experience.
d. He pioneered modern psychology's method of introspection.

121. Consider the following graphic. Which sociological concept does the graphic best illustrate?

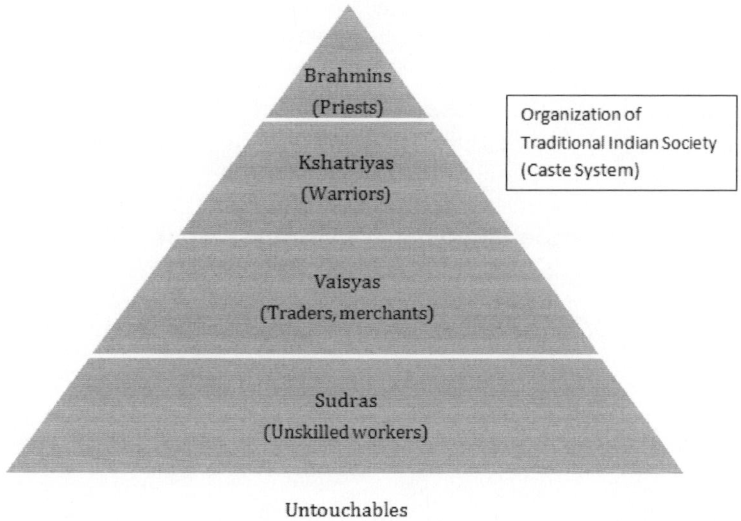

a. Assimilation
b. Stratification
c. Diffusion
d. Socialization

122. According to John Locke's social contract theory, a central reason human beings enter social contracts is:

a. To delegate the right to punish to certain individuals
b. Because social contracts provide the basis for moral behavior
c. To establish natural rights for citizens
d. Because the state of nature is nasty, brutish, and short

123. In social sciences, reification is best understood as:

a. Using qualitative data instead of quantitative data
b. Treating an abstraction as a concrete thing
c. The use of heuristic devices
d. Mistaking subjectivity for objectivity

124. Suppose that every time a cat hears a can opener, it is fed. The cat runs to the kitchen to be fed every time it hears a can opener. In psychology, this kind of association is called:

a. Operant conditioning
b. Habituation
c. Classical conditioning
d. Conformity

125. Which of the following best describes a main difference between anthropology and psychology?

a. Anthropology involves natural science; psychology does not.
b. Anthropology focuses on humans as a species; psychology focuses more on humans as individuals.
c. Anthropology uses primarily quantitative research methods; psychology does not.
d. Anthropology focuses only on the physical evolution of the human species; psychology focuses on human behavior.

126. Most of the earliest civilizations flourished in or near what sort of geographic feature?

a. Mountains
b. Valleys
c. Oceans
d. Rivers

127. Which statement best describes the role of natural selection in Charles Darwin's theory of evolution?

a. Natural selection describes the diversity of environmental pressures.
b. Natural selection is the process by which individual organisms adapt.
c. Natural selection explains how organisms inherit acquired characteristics.
d. Natural selection is the mechanism by which species are said to evolve.

128. Which is the best description for how cognitive psychologists seek to uncover and explain individual differences between humans?

a. By studying how society influences a person's beliefs
b. By studying the ways in which people know and think
c. By studying how people struggle with emotional conflicts
d. By studying human biology as it relates to behavior

129. The concept of checks and balances is evident in which of the following?

a. Federal judiciary appeals
b. Presidential veto
c. States' rights
d. The House and the Senate

130. In his 1905 special theory of relativity, Albert Einstein postulated which of the following?

a. A unified field theory
b. A mathematical definition of gravity
c. The relativity of the speed of light
d. That there is no absolute simultaneity

Answer Key and Explanations for Test #2

1. C: Measles was the latest epidemic listed to attack the Incas, in 1618. The earliest was smallpox (B), which killed half the Taíno population of Hispaniola (now Haiti and the Dominican Republic) in 1518 and virtually wiped out the Aztecs in Tenochtitlan (now Mexico City) by 1521. Smallpox killed an estimated 60-90% of the Incas by the 1520s, with repeated epidemics in 1558 and 1589. An epidemic of typhus (A) in 1546 caused more deaths among the Incas. The 1558 smallpox epidemic was accompanied by an epidemic of influenza, killing even more Incas. An epidemic of diphtheria (D) added to the death toll in 1614. The measles epidemic of 1618 (C) attacked the remnants of the Inca culture. European colonizers unwittingly imported these diseases. Since the Europeans had developed antibodies to the infections through many years of exposure, it never occurred to them that the Native Americans had no such exposure and hence no immunity. This lack of immune defenses made the diseases much more virulent to the Indians than they had ever been to the Europeans who carried them. As a result, a majority of Native Americans died from diseases introduced by Europeans.

2. C: The male passengers of the Mayflower signed the Compact after a disagreement regarding where in the Americas they should establish a colony. The Compact served as a written basis for laws in their subsequent colony. Because the Mayflower Compact did not list particular rights, it is not best understood as a blueprint for the Bill of Rights. This eliminates choice B. Though the Compact did in part serve as a basis for government, it did not declare independence from King James; its last line, for example, specifically refers to King James as the writers' sovereign. This eliminates choice A. Finally, although the Mayflower Compact does include religious language, it is a brief document that does not detail, defend, or establish as official any particular religious doctrine, including Puritan religious doctrine. This eliminates choice D.

3. C: Pennsylvania is most closely associated with William Penn, a Quaker of the Society of Friends. Penn hoped to establish a colony where Quakers would be free to practice their religion. This colony offered religious tolerance toward many other religions as well; Dutch Mennonites and German Baptists were among those who came to Pennsylvania. The desire for freedom of the press was not a salient concern in the motivation for colonizing Pennsylvania; this eliminates option A. Although some European colonists came to Pennsylvania for economic reasons, these are not best understood in terms of escaping high taxes or trade restrictions. This eliminates options B and D.

4. B: Peter Zenger was an 18th century journalist in New York who was charged with seditious libel after he published articles critical of New York governor William Cosby. His subsequent acquittal in 1735 established a precedent for American freedom of the press. Options A, C, and D can all be rejected because they do not accurately describe the historical significance of Peter Zenger's trial. Although these options name other important freedoms or rights in American history, these rights or freedoms were not central to Peter Zenger's trial. In particular, note that while answers B, C, and D all list rights contained in the First Amendment to the United States Constitution, only B contains the particular right at issue in the Zenger case.

5. A: The Navigation Acts in the seventeenth and eighteenth centuries restricted commercial activity in the American colonies and resulted in the constraint of manufacturing. The Acts were a logical extension of British mercantilism, a view according to which the colonies existed primarily to benefit Great Britain. Answer B can be rejected because one Navigation Act forced the colonists to buy more expensive sugar from the British West Indies, rather than the French West Indies. Option C can be eliminated because a positive result of the Navigation Acts was giving the American colonists a monopoly on tobacco by restricting tobacco production in Great Britain itself. Option D can be eliminated because the Acts did not place a tax on shipping goods to Great Britain.

6. B: The cost of the French and Indian War was high, and after the war, Great Britain sought to have the American colonies help pay for the war through measures such as higher taxes. This led to colonial resentment, in part because the colonists lacked representation in the British government. Option A can be rejected because, rather than limiting oversight on the American colonies, Great Britain reasserted its authority there. The Proclamation of 1763, although it did limit the location of new American colonies, was modified in response to colonial demands prior to the American Revolution. This eliminates choice C. Option D can be rejected because the French and Indian War (in which American colonists participated) actually decreased colonial dependence on the British military.

7. A: Central to the Manifest Destiny (the belief that it was the right and duty of the United States to expand its borders) was the belief that the United States had a duty to spread democracy, offering a democratic example to the rest of the world. Option B was much less significant; proponents of the Manifest Destiny were more interested in spreading what they regarded as civilization than in spreading material prosperity in particular. Option C can be rejected because the issue of slavery was controversial; some proponents of the Manifest Destiny were decided supporters of slavery and others were not. Option D can be rejected because religious freedom was not a central issue for proponents of Manifest Destiny.

8. C: Under the Treaty of Guadalupe Hidalgo, the United States acquired modern-day California, Nevada, Utah, New Mexico; in addition, the United States also acquired parts of present-day Arizona, Colorado, Oklahoma, Kansas and Wyoming. Options A, B, and D can each be rejected because they leave out some part of land acquired by the United States through the treaty. Under the Treaty of Guadalupe Hidalgo, Mexico lost over half of its territory. The United States agreed to pay Mexico $15 million for damage incurred in Mexico during the US-Mexican War and to respect Mexican land grants; however, when the US Congress ratified the treaty, it deleted the latter provision.

9. D: The Battle of Chapultepec, a citadel outside Mexico City, was last major US assault prior to the US capture of Mexico City. When the United States won the battle, the Mexican defensive line collapsed, leaving the way open for US troops to march on the Mexican capital. The assault on Chapultepec was organized by US General Winfield Scott; although General Zachary Taylor was considered an American hero due in part to his performance during the US-Mexican War, this was not because of any involvement with the Battle of Chapultepec. This eliminates option A. Because the US won the battle, option B can be rejected. General Santa Ana was not personally involved in the battle, eliminating option C.

10. C: In his March to the Sea, General Sherman sought to make both civilians and soldiers experience the brutal hardships of war in order to weaken their will to fight, thereby undermining the Confederate war effort itself. Sherman accomplished this through burning crops and killing livestock. Option A does not describe a primary goal of the March and can be rejected on that basis. Although a secondary motivation might have been to distract Lee, at the time of Sherman's march, Lee's troops were engaged with Grant's forces in Virginia, not Maryland. This eliminates option B. Option D can be eliminated because Sherman's primary intention was not to liberate slaves (although slaves were in fact liberated during the march).

11. A: After a series of disagreements over Reconstruction Policy, Congress passed the Tenure of Office Act, according to which the President needed congressional consent to dismiss from office anyone who had been confirmed by the Senate. President Johnson violated the Act by dismissing Secretary of War Edwin Stanton, whom radical Republicans wanted to keep in office. Congress accordingly impeached President Johnson. Regarding option B, Southern states did enact "Black Laws" to prevent African Americans from voting, but President Johnson was not impeached because he allowed such laws (and thus failed to enforce the Fourteenth Amendment). Johnson did seek to disenfranchise former Confederate officers, and he did attempt to form a third political party; but neither of these actions were grounds for his impeachment (with respect to the former action, radical Republicans were in agreement). This eliminates choices C and D respectively.

12. D: As a result of the Spanish-American War, the United States became a more powerful nation. At the war's end, Spain ceded Guam and Puerto Rico to the United States, and the United States purchased the Philippines for $20 million. Answer A can be rejected because, though the United States Navy represented itself very well throughout the war, the United States Army was plagued by inefficiency. Answer B can be rejected because Spain was the first nation in the conflict to issue a formal declaration of war. This is true in spite of the fact that Spain's declaration of war came in part as a response to American actions. Answer C can be rejected because the sinking of the Maine did not cast doubts on the US Navy. Rather, the US Navy defeated Spanish ships rather handily.

13. D: Advances in technology were applied not only to industrial production, but also to farming machinery. Farmers could then supply larger amounts of food to urban workers at lower prices. Farming was not abandoned in favor of industry (A). The many additional workers in cities needed food that they did not grow, so there was an even greater market for farming. This did not mean that farming took precedence over industry (B). Both fields increased during the 19th century, and they complemented one another. Specialization and mechanization were processes applied to both farming and industry. At this time, they were not applied more to farming (C) or industry.

14. C: A central plank in the platform of the Populist Party was free coinage of silver, which allowed citizens to exchange their silver at US mints for US currency. This platform was subsequently adopted by the Democratic Party and was a major domestic issue in the 1892 and 1896 presidential elections. The heart of the issue was the standard on which US currency would be based. Option A can be rejected because the Populist Party was formed in part by farmers unhappy about the decreasing cost of farm crops; the elevation of these costs contributed to the dissolution of the Populist Party. Options B and D can both be rejected because neither were influential planks in the platform of the Populist Party.

15. D: During the Vietnam War, a central aim of the United States was to prevent the spread of communism. At the time of the war, North Vietnamese communist forces threatened South Vietnam, and the United States came to the aid of the South Vietnamese government. The Domino Theory of communism held that one nation's conversion to communism was likely to lead to other nations in that region also converting to communism. The aim of the United States was essentially negative (to stop communism) rather than positive (to implement a specific kind of democracy). This eliminates option A. Option B and C can both be rejected because neither describes the primary aim of US involvement in Vietnam in the 1960s and 1970s. While options A, B, and C could have been incidental benefits obtained by fighting North Vietnam, none correctly state the primary goal of the US.

16. B: After World War I, the United States passed the Immigration Act of 1924, which regulated the number of immigrants in part according to their national origin. The United States sought to avoid the problems of Europe and other nations by limiting the number of foreigners who entered the United States. Option A can be rejected because quite soon after World War I, both inflation and unemployment were significant problems in the United States. Option C can be rejected because in the years immediately following World War I, the United States did not build its navy even to the extent allowed by treaty. Finally, option D can be rejected because after World War I, the United States made arrangements for the US to have access to oil in Colombia and in Middle Eastern countries.

17. A: The author's main point in the passage is that people should consider what justifies the use of deadly weapons on civilians using the historical case of the bombing of Hiroshima and Nagasaki as the central reference. Both the opening and concluding sentences concern citizens and reflection, or examination, while the middle of the passage offers historical facts to illustrate an alternative and lesser-known reason for the bombing. All this suggests that option A correctly describes the main idea of the passage. Option B can be rejected because the author, rather than stating that the use of such weapons is not justified, instead raises the question of when it is and urges the importance of asking this question. Option C can be rejected because the author does not make that general claim; option D describes a more minor idea expressed in the passage.

18. A: Henry Kissinger, US Secretary of State from 1973-1977 and National Security Adviser from 1969-1965, helped negotiate two agreements related to the arms race between the United States and the Soviet Union. According to one such agreement, SALT I (from the Strategic Arms Limitation Talks), the US and Soviet Union agreed to limit the number of offensive strategic missiles. Kissinger also helped to establish a cease-fire in the Arab-Israeli War in 1973, and he was also involved in a bombing campaign in Laos and Cambodia. However, neither of these events influenced the course of the Cold War to the degree to which the arms agreements did. Answers B and D respectively may thus be eliminated. Answer C can be rejected because Kissinger did attempt to involve the Soviet Union in US efforts to end the Vietnam War.

19. A: In exchange for the removal of Soviet Cuban missile launching sites, which were under construction at the time of the crisis, President Khrushchev sought a pledge from the United States that the United States would not invade Cuba. Khrushchev also demanded that the United States close its missile launching sites located in Turkey, not on an island off the Soviet coast. This eliminates option B. The Soviet Union did not demand either an apology from the United States as a condition for the removal of the launching sites, or negotiations regarding the production of nuclear weapons. This eliminates options C and D.

20. C: The 1944 G.I. Bill offered several significant benefits for US veterans. These included economic assistance for veterans to attend college, mortgage subsidies, and unemployment benefits. Over a million veterans took advantage of the opportunity to attend college, and many homes were built with support provided by the G.I. Bill. This increase in home ownership and the availability of higher education contributed to the creation of a new middle class. The Bill did not offer veterans specific incentives for staying in the military after World War II; this eliminates option A. It did not offer free housing for veterans; this eliminates option B. Finally, the Bill did not privilege veterans in the work force; this eliminates option D.

21. A: Jonas Salk's polio vaccine prevented thousands of new cases of polio in a nation which had become accustomed to the ravages of the disease. The invention was a major innovation that affected Americans all over the United States, as children were vaccinated against the disease. Unfortunately, Salk's vaccine did cause polio in a small number of children; however, option B can be rejected because this had less of an impact than the near eradication of the disease in the United States. Option C can be rejected because, although Salk's manner of announcing the vaccine ruffled the feathers of some of his scientist peers, it did not ignite a widespread or public debate regarding the media and science. Finally, option D can be rejected because it is simply false.

22. D: Under the New Deal, the federal government created the Federal Deposit Insurance Corporation to insure bank deposits. Option A can be eliminated because, although the Public Works Administration was a component of the New Deal, it was concerned with providing work to Americans through projects such as the construction of dams and bridges. Answer B can be eliminated because Roosevelt did not require banks to loan money at certain interest rates, and option C can be rejected because Roosevelt did not attempt to shift ownership of prominent banks to the federal government.

23. C: Sit-ins were peaceful protests during which both African-American and Caucasian participants protested segregated, or "whites-only," businesses by sitting at such establishments and asking to be served. These protests led to the integration of lunch counters and other businesses. In 1954, the Supreme Court ruled in *Brown v. Board of Education* that public schools could not be separate and equal; this ruling occurred independently of sit-ins. This eliminates choice D. The sit-ins did not focus on either integration of the armed forces, or on literacy tests as requirements for voter registration. Though reforms regarding these issues were passed, they were not directly a result of sit-ins. This eliminates choices A and B respectively.

24. A: While Martin Luther King is famous for his advocacy of nonviolence, Malcolm X defended self-defense against aggression by white people. In the course of his work, King did indeed mobilize ordinary citizens; however, Malcolm X did not focus on working with local white political leaders, but instead focused on black communities. This eliminates option B. Malcolm X also sometimes spoke against black citizens practicing Christianity, linking the practice of that religion in part to oppression; this eliminates option C. Finally, option D can be rejected because King did not promote Black Nationalism, while Malcolm X did.

25. D: Under the War Powers Act of 1973, the President can send combat troops to battle (or to an area where hostilities are imminent) for only 60 days, with the possibility of extending this period of time to 90 days. In order to keep deployed troops in place (or to send additional troops) after this period of time has elapsed, the President must seek Congressional approval, either in the form of a mandate or in the form of a declaration of war. Option A can be eliminated because Congress was responsible for approving war-related funding prior to the War Powers Act, which did not affect this responsibility. Neither option B nor option C accurately describes the importance of the War Powers Act.

26. A: The Supreme Court decision in *Gibbons v. Ogden* ruled that Congress has the power to regulate interstate commerce via the Constitution's Commerce Clause. The decision in *Ableman v. Booth* (B) ruled that State courts cannot rule to contradict Federal court rulings. The decision in *Plessy v. Ferguson* (C) ruled that "separate but equal" segregation was constitutional. The decision in The *Paquete Habana* (D) ruled that customary international law could be used as a reference by Federal courts because it is integrated as part of American law. Except for choice A, none of these other decisions specifically involved regulating interstate navigation.

27. D: The Equal Rights Amendment, though it was approved by Congress in 1972 (C), was not ratified in its deadline year for ratification of 1983. The amendment fell short of reaching ratification by just three states' votes. President Reagan did appoint judge Sandra Day O'Connor, the first female justice, to the Supreme Court (A), despite the fact that in general, he and his administration were against feminist agendas (B).

28. A: The Nile River flooded regularly and reliably, irrigating the crops of the ancient Egyptians. This best explains the stability of Egyptian culture. Answer (B) can be rejected because though the Nile River is expansive; its size did not prevent the Egyptian people from settling elsewhere.

Answer (C) can be rejected because the Valley of the Kings, an ancient Egyptian city, did not separate Upper and Lower Egypt. Answer (D) can be rejected because, even if true, interaction with other cultures is more likely to lead to a dynamic, changing culture than a stable, unchanging culture.

29. D: Ziggurats were towers dedicated to gods; their prevalence indicates the importance of religion in Mesopotamian culture. The other options can be rejected because they pair accurate facts about Mesopotamia with inaccurate summaries of the purposes of the ziggurats. For example, while rulers of Mesopotamian cities fought among themselves, ziggurats were not used as lookouts. This eliminates option A. Although astrology was practiced in Mesopotamia, ziggurats did not function as places for stargazing or observing the sky. Finally, Mesopotamian cities were ruled by kings, but the ziggurats were not dedicated to them. This eliminates options B and C.

30. D: Arabic mathematicians, such as the ninth-century mathematician al-Khwarizmi, made important contributions to algebra; the term "algebra" itself derives from a work of al-Khwarizmi's. However, Arabic algebra did not recognize negative numbers; this eliminates option B. Option C can be rejected because probability was developed initially by French mathematicians Blaise Pascal and Pierre de Fermat. Option A can be rejected because modern calculus (building on earlier foundations) is usually taken to have begun (separately) in the works of Isaac Newton and Gottfried Leibniz.

31. C: This is the best choice because Athenian culture developed more than a thousand years later than Minoan. The remaining choices all reflect true statements, so none is the best choice for the question. The legendary King Minos is the namesake for the island. Knossos was the center of Minoan culture and its capital was on the island of Crete. The capital was a mazelike structure from which we derive the term "labyrinth." Many frescoes, or wall paintings, have been uncovered and reconstructed provide scholars a great source of information about Minoan culture.

32. A: The word "democracy" comes from two Greek root words: *demos* "people" and *kratia* "rule."

33. C: The cultural developments that did not occur before the 15th century were the Baroque style in the arts (music, visual arts, architecture) and the founding of the Jesuit order. The Baroque arts were encouraged by the Church during the Counter-Reformation, which occurred following the beginning of the Protestant Reformation as a reaction against it, in the 16th century. In addition, the Jesuit order was formed during this time (as well as other religious orders such as the Theatines and the Barnabites). The Jesuits quickly assumed a leading role in educating people during the Counter-Reformation. Romanesque architecture (A) developed out of the influence of the Catholic Church between circa 1000 AD and circa 1300 AD, when it was succeeded by the Gothic style (B), also influenced by the Church and its cathedrals. The Catholic Church also sponsored most of the great artists of the Renaissance (D), including Michelangelo, Leonardo Da Vinci, Raphael, Botticelli, Bernini, Titian, Caravaggio, Tintoretto, Fra Angelico and their famous paintings and sculptures, during the 14th and 15th centuries. The Catholic Church was also responsible for the development of European classical music because Catholic monks pioneered the first modern system of musical notation in order to standardize religious music the world over. This innovation not only allowed for the composition of a vast body of liturgical music, but also it contributed to the development of secular classical music in Europe.

34. B: Although Charlemagne himself may not have believed his authority was conferred by the pope, Charlemagne's successors sometimes used the title "Holy Roman Emperor" (given to them by the pope) as a basis for their authority. Thus, the title "Holy Roman Emperor" strengthened the notion that political authority was conferred by the pope. Charlemagne united much of Europe under a single ruler prior to being named Holy Roman Emperor. While Catholicism may have been the recognized religion, the naming of Charlemagne as Holy Roman Emperor did not make it so. After being so named, Charlemagne did not renounce his conquests. This eliminates options A, C, and D respectively.

35. C: Under the Western European feudal system, rulers granted vassals land in exchange for military and political service. Although the right to use land would often pass from father to son, it was not on the basis of blood relations that a ruler granted land to a vassal; this eliminates option B. Religious institutions such as monasteries did indeed own land, but did not own most of it, eliminating option A. Finally, feudalism was a land-based economy that made a shift from a spice-based economy to a gold-based economy. Therefore, option D can be eliminated.

36. D: Power was centralized in the Incan Empire. When the invading Spaniards imprisoned Incan ruler Atahualpa and killed other Incan military leaders, the Incas were unable to mount an effective military response. Incas of lesser status simply lacked the appropriate authority. Answers A and B may be eliminated because they are factually inaccurate. The Incas had built some functional roads, which allowed the invading Spanish to access some Incan cities. Also, Pizarro's soldiers did not outnumber the Incans. The new diseases introduced by the Spanish decimated the Incan army, making D the correct answer. While the centralized power structure did create a vulnerability, the impact of disease was far more devastating.

37. D: The Triple Alliance allowed the city-states to conquer city-states and land by combining forces against mutual enemies. The Triple Alliance and its conquered areas are commonly thought of as the Aztec Empire. While some conquered areas did rebel against the Aztec Empire at the time the Spanish conquistadores arrived, such rebellion did not specifically concern the city-states of the Triple Alliance. Texcoco and Tlacopan did not use the Alliance as a front against Tenochtitlan. The Triple Alliance had nothing to do with the number of annual human sacrifices. This eliminates options A, B, and C.

38. B: Akbar allowed the practice of both Hinduism and Islam, despite pressure from Islamic religious leaders to do otherwise. Akbar specifically permitted the construction of Hindu temples, which freed Akbar from Hindu resistance that he might otherwise have faced. This fact eliminates answer D. Breaking from some past practices, Akbar also used cash instead of land to pay empire officials, allowing him to control more land. Because of this, option A can be rejected. Option C can be rejected because Akbar allowed certain defeated princes to keep their lands.

39. A: In the 1780s, the French national debt was very high. The French nobility adamantly resisted attempts by King Louis XVI to reform tax laws, which led to a high tax burden on the French peasantry. The French government spent almost 50% of its national expenditures on debt-related payments during the 1780s; thus, it could not and did not spend almost 70% to finance luxuries for the French nobility. This eliminates choice B. King Louis XVI temporarily banned the guild system to bolster, rather than stifle, free trade. Because this system gave skilled craftsmen economic advantages, journeymen opposed ending the system. This eliminates choice D. Regardless of the status of guilds before the French Revolution, French society did not offer many opportunities for upward social mobility. Few peasants were able to advance. This eliminates choice C.

40. A: Joan of Arc was a French peasant who had visions of saints telling her to lead the French army in an attack against the English. She eventually led the French to a victorious battle against the English in 1429. Several years later she was brought before the Inquisition by political enemies, found guilty of heresy, and sentenced to death.

41. A: Russian involvement in World War I brought social tension in Russia to a head. Contributing factors included military defeats and civilian suffering. Prior to Russia entering the war, Russian factory workers could legally strike, but during the war, it was illegal for them to act collectively. This eliminates answer C. Protests continued during World War I, and the Russian government was overthrown in 1917. This eliminates answer D. Answer B can be rejected because World War I did not go well for the Russian Army; Nicholas III, therefore, had no successes upon which to capitalize.

42. B: Many Americans migrated during World War II, seeking work in war-related factories; boomtowns sprang up as a result. Some Japanese-Americans served in the United States military during World War II; in fact, the all-Japanese 442nd Regimental Combat Team was decorated by the US government for its service. This eliminates choice D. Answer C can be rejected because Caucasian and African-American soldiers served in segregated units. Answer A can be eliminated because consumption actually increased in postwar American society, as production was high and returning US soldiers had income to spend.

43. D: The Truman Doctrine was intended to prevent Greece and Turkey from becoming communist countries. However, its broad language had implications beyond those two nations, suggesting that US policy generally should be to aid people who resisted outside forces attempting to impose communist rule. This doctrine led to US involvement in Korea and Vietnam, where US forces fought against communist forces in those nations. The United States did have a plan for assisting the European economies, but it was the Marshall Plan, not the Truman Doctrine. This eliminates choice B. While President Truman did establish a President's Committee on Civil Rights, it was not as a result of the Truman Doctrine. This eliminates answer A. Finally, when inflation plagued the postwar US economy, the federal government took measures to address inflation and other economic issues, rather than steering clear of them. This eliminates choice C.

44. B: The Supreme Court decided the case of *Montejo v. Louisiana* in 2009; therefore, this case represents the only listed decision to occur after the Cold War ended in 1991. In this case, the Supreme Court ruled that a defendant might waive the right to counsel for police interrogation, even if that interrogation was initiated after the defendant asserted that right at an arraignment or other proceeding. This decision overruled the ruling in *Michigan v. Jackson* (1986). The decision in *Gideon v. Wainwright* (A) was made in 1963, and ruled that any person charged with a serious criminal offense had the right to an attorney and to be provided one if they could not afford it. The 1964 decision in *Escobedo v. Illinois* (C) ruled that a person in police custody had the right to consult an attorney. The 1966 decision in *Miranda v. Arizona* (D) ruled that police must inform suspects of their rights to remain silent, to have a lawyer, to be appointed a lawyer if they cannot afford one, and for interrogation to stop if they invoke their right to remain silent. After this case, these rights have been commonly referred to as "Miranda rights," and arrests or interrogations wherein police do not "Mirandize" or inform suspects of these rights can be thrown out for not following procedure.

45. B: Johann Gutenberg's printing press led to increased scientific knowledge and advancement as scientific texts were printed and dispersed throughout Europe. Because the distribution of such texts extended outside of Germany, options C and D may be eliminated. Gutenberg Bibles were printed using Gutenberg's press, and thus Gutenberg's invention was likely a factor in the Reformation of the Catholic Church. In fact, Martin Luther's Ninety-Five Theses (against the Catholic Church) were printed using a printing press. However, this reformation occurred alongside, rather than in place of, the advancement of scientific knowledge. This eliminates option A.

46. A: According to Plato's Theory of Forms, nonphysical ideal forms are most good and real. The form of the Good has the highest degree of reality and goodness. Answer B can be rejected because Plato did not believe there was an ideal form of evil. Answer C can be rejected because Plato did not believe the Good formed a trinity with other forms. Answer D can be rejected because, though Plato advocated Socratic reasoning as a method for coming to know the forms, he did not believe such reasoning led to redemption from sin as Christian doctrine contemplates this notion.

47. A: The Catholic Church was both powerful and wealthy in medieval Europe. It affected the lives of both the rich and poor; for example, wealthy families often donated to monasteries in exchange for prayers on the donors' behalf. This eliminates option B. Because of these donations, some monasteries became quite wealthy. Rather than being a neutral force, the Catholic Church wielded political power. In medieval times, some claimed that rulers derived their authority to rule from the Catholic Church itself. These facts eliminate options C and D.

48. A: The Crusades' biggest impact upon Europe's Jewish population was that entire Jewish communities were killed during the First Crusade. This is the only option that accurately describes historical effects of the Crusades on the Jewish population. Rather than diminishing anti-Jewish sentiment, the Crusades seemed to inflame it, eliminating option B. One specific example of Crusades-era anti-Semitism is that many Jewish people were excluded from particular trades, and thus did not profit from the Crusades. This fact eliminates option C. Finally, there were no Jewish-only battalions during the Crusades, eliminating option D.

49. C: With its emphasis on an individual's relationship with God and personal responsibility for salvation, the religious reformation sparked by Martin Luther in 1517 contributed to a rise in individualism. Rather than weakening the civil authorities in Europe, the Reformation served to strengthen many secular authorities by undermining the authority of the Catholic Church. This eliminates answer B. Although the Reformation deemphasized the Virgin Mary, it influenced improvements to education for women and girls, particularly in Germany. This eliminates answer A. Finally, option D can be rejected because the Catholic Church underwent its own internal reformation, in part due to Luther's Reformation.

50. C: Although options A, B, and D all describe important factors in the Neolithic Revolution, option C—the ability of communities to stockpile surplus food—is the factor most directly responsibility for the rise of trade practices. Communities were thus able to trade surplus food for other goods and services, a societal feature not present in hunter-gatherer societies. Option A, the ability of people to better choose where they lived (because they could carry the portable tools of agriculture with them to make a place habitable) contributed to the spread of agriculture, but less directly to the rise of trade practices. New advances in tools also contributed less directly to the rise of trade, as did the rise of new religious practices. These facts eliminate answers D and B, respectively.

51. A: In a departure from classical painting, Cubists painted their subjects as though from multiple perspectives rather than from a single perspective, as though to reflect the increasingly complex world of the 20th century. This approach to painting included paintings of the human body; the paintings therefore sometimes seemed to distort the human body rather than elevate it or regard it as sacrosanct. This eliminates option B. Cubism favored rationality over emotion in that it involved breaking up subjects along geometric planes; this eliminates option C. Finally, option D can be rejected because Cubist paintings often utilized tame, mild colors, rather than bright, vivid ones.

52. D: The West Bank contains a number of significant natural water reserves (aquifers). These aquifers are an important source of water not only to the Palestinians living in the West Bank but to Israel as well. Access to these aquifers is a significant motivation to Israel's continuing control of the

West Bank. The West Bank does not border the Mediterranean Sea; this eliminates option A. There are no significant oil reserves in the West Bank; this eliminates option B. Though there are olive groves in the West Bank, olives and olive products are far less important resources to Israel than water.

53. C: Women, including notable women's rights activists such as Susan B. Anthony, figured importantly in the temperance movement of the 19th century in the United States. Many women were motivated not only by the association of saloons with gambling and prostitution, but by the association of alcohol and domestic violence. Lost productivity was a concern held by figures such as Henry Ford, but figured less prominently with respect to women's role in the temperance movement. This eliminates option B. Option D, infertility, was not a motivating factor. Regarding option A, some women's rights activists were also concerned about race relations and racial injustice, but a specific concern about racial violence was not a primary motivating factor behind the drive for temperance.

54. A: When the President sent federal troops, this caused the Whiskey Rebellion to end, which resolved the situation and added to the new government's credibility. It did not result in a setback for the government. It is true that the whiskey tax was central to Hamilton's revenue program (B). It is true that farmers in western states, including Pennsylvania, did not want to pay this tax (C). It is also true that in addition to objecting to the tax and refusing to pay it, a group of farmers in Pennsylvania terrorized tax collectors to make their point (D). It is true that Washington responded to the farmers' terrorism by sending around 15,000 soldiers to quell the Whiskey Rebellion in 1794.

55. A: Most of the conquered peoples were not granted Roman citizenship. Each conquered state was allowed some degree of cultural autonomy. Subjects were expected to follow the laws of Rome, pay taxes, and hand over land and supplies to the Roman government.

56. C: The main subject matter of civic responsibility is a person's responsibilities as a citizen. By contrast, the main subject matter of personal responsibility is one's responsibilities as a person. For example, keeping a promise to a friend is often a matter of personal responsibility because such a duty arises from the friendship. Serving on a jury when called to do so is an example of civic responsibility because such a duty arises from the person's citizenship. None of the other options given accurately describe the main subject matter of civic responsibility. For example, while a journalist might see accurate reporting of government actions as his or her civic responsibility, such reporting is not the main subject matter of civic responsibility and is also a responsibility that arises from that journalist's employment. Similar reasoning applies to a person's responsibilities as a government worker. This eliminates options A and D. Civic responsibility does not primarily concern inter-government relations; this eliminates option B.

57. D: A practical application of content learned involves action, not merely knowledge. Options A and C, although they describe content that students would reasonably learn in a class or unit on the structure of the US government, do not describe applications of content, or applications of a social studies education. Therefore, options A and C can both be rejected. Option B does involve action and not merely the acquisition of knowledge. However, it is not as directly tied to learning the structure of the US government as option D, informed participation in US political processes. This is because informed participation in school elections is quite possible without knowing the structure of the U.S government. Informed participation in US political processes requires knowledge of the structure of the US government (i.e., voting on an issue requires an understanding of where a given candidate stands on that issue).

58. B: Published in early 1776, *Common Sense* condemned hereditary kingship. The pamphlet was popular in Colonial America, and even George Washington noticed its effect on the general population. Later that same year, Jefferson drafted the Declaration of Independence.

59. B: Under the Fifth Amendment to the U.S. Constitution, the government may not strip certain basic rights from citizens without following the law. In the language of the Fifth Amendment itself, a person shall not "be deprived of life, liberty, or property without due process of law." Of all the options, option B is the only one that accurately describes the concept of due process as understood in the Fifth Amendment. Because due process does not explicitly guarantee a trial by jury within a reasonable timeframe, nor equal protection under the law (concepts covered elsewhere in the Constitution), options A and C can be rejected. Option D can be rejected because the Constitution restricts the government's ability to take away certain rights without following the law, not without a "dire cause" (such as the threat of imminent attack).

60. B: President John Adams appointed William Marbury as Justice of the Peace, but Secretary of State James Madison never delivered the commission. Marbury claimed that under the Judiciary Act of 1789, the Supreme Court could order his commission be given to him. The Supreme Court denied Marbury's petition citing that the Judiciary Act of 1789 was unconstitutional, although they believed he was entitled to his commission.

61. C: A federalist system of government is a government under which power is shared by a central authority and sub-components of the federation. In the United States in particular, power is shared by the federal government and the individual states. Option A, that the legislative branch consists of two representative bodies (the House of Representatives and the Senate) is true, of course, but does not describe a uniquely federalist structure. Rather, it describes the concept of bicameralism. Option A may thus be eliminated. Option B, likewise, describes different types of democracy but not federalism. Option B can thus be eliminated. Regarding option D, this statement is also true (the US Constitution shapes national legislation) but it is not a descriptive statement of the federalist system because the statement makes no mention that power is shared by the states.

62. D: After the American Revolution, the framers of the American government were concerned that a strong central government could lead to abuses of power. Accordingly, The Articles of Confederation did not grant the federal government the ability to raise taxes. Another restriction was the inability to regulate interstate commerce. Options A, B, and C can all be eliminated because, though the federal government was generally weak under the Articles of Confederation, the Articles granted the federal government each of the powers given in those options.

63. C: Prior to the Seventeenth Amendment, adopted in 1913, US senators were chosen by state legislatures rather than by popular state elections. The former system caused problems beginning in the mid-nineteenth century, problems exacerbated by the fact that there was no consistent process among the states for just how state legislatures chose their US Senators. The Seventeenth Amendment required that US Senators be chosen by direct popular election by the citizens of the relevant state. The Seventeenth Amendment did not concern state senators (i.e., senators serving state Senates), governors, or censuses to determine the appropriate level of representation in a House of Representatives. This eliminates options A, B, and D.

64. C: Line 3 best lists the kinds of cases over which the US federal court system has jurisdiction. The US federal court system has jurisdiction over cases involving constitutional law, bankruptcy, and disputes between states (the federal court system also has jurisdiction over cases concerning US treaties and laws, among other types of cases). State courts have jurisdiction over most contract cases, most criminal cases, and most personal injury cases; this eliminates Line 1, Line 2, and Line 4, each of which list one of those kinds of cases as under the jurisdiction of the US federal court system.

65. C: State and federal courts issue subpoenas for court cases, and Congress has the right to subpoena experts and witnesses for congressional investigations. Failure to respond to a subpoena from either Congress or the judiciary has consequences that could include incarceration.

66. C: The US Supreme Court decision in *Plessy v. Ferguson* affirmed the state of Louisiana's constitutional right to offer "separate but equal" accommodations on railway lines within that state. The decision provided a legal basis for racial segregation in US society, including segregation in education and other public services. Option A can be rejected because the primary importance of the ruling was less to reinforce state's rights than to affirm the supposed legality of segregation. The decision produced increasingly significant consequences as US society continued to segregate. *Plessy v. Ferguson* did not address poll taxes or the legality of railway strikes; this eliminates options B and D.

67. B: The President has the authority to grant pardons and clemencies for federal crimes, except in cases of impeachment. The House elects the Speaker of the House, the President serves two terms, and Congress declares war.

68. B: The Electoral College officially elects the President and the Vice President. The number of electors, or Electoral College members, allotted to a state is equal to that state's total number of US Senators and US Representatives. A state with two US Senators and one US Representative, for example, would have three electors in the Electoral College. Because every state has two US Senators and at least one US Representative, every state has at least three electors in the Electoral College. Option B is the only option that correctly describes how a state's number of Electoral College voters is determined; neither the number of counties in a state, nor the number of State Secretaries is relevant to this number.

69. C: In statistical analysis, the range is the difference between the highest value and the smallest value within a given set of data. Here, the highest value for voter participation in Cedar Valley is 67%, and the smallest value is 42%. The difference between these two is 25, so the range here is 25. Option C is the only answer that correctly gives the range for this set of data; options B and D express a span of numbers but not the range in the statistical sense; they can therefore be rejected. Option D does not give a difference between the largest and smallest values and can therefore be rejected.

70. B: According to the chart, the median for voter participation in Cedar Valley is 55%. In general, the median is the value in the "center"—it is the middle value within a set of values that are arranged in ascending or descending order. For example, in a set of values consisting of 2, 3, 6, 7, and 10, the median is 6. Option A gives the mean (or average) for voter participation, not the median. Options C and D do not give the median, either, and can therefore be rejected.

71. C: The Federalist Party advocated a pro-British foreign policy and therefore opposed the War of 1812. This made the Federalists unpopular with many Americans; this unpopularity deepened when the war ended after several American victories. The Federalist Party did advocate a strong central government; however, this position was not a key factor in the Party's decline. This eliminates option D. Option A can be rejected because the Federalist Party did organize state political parties in states such as Connecticut, Delaware, and Maryland. Many members of the Federalist Party were pro-trade and pro-business, as many members were well-to-do businessmen. This eliminates option B.

72. A: The Iroquois Confederacy was a confederacy of originally five (and later six) Native American Tribes, founded in 1570. Many decisions involved compromise between two sets of Lords from different tribes, analogous to the compromise involved in decision-making between the US House of Representatives and the US Senate. For the Confederacy to accept a decision, Mohawk and Seneca Lords needed to come to an agreement with Oneida and Cayuga Lords. Option B can be rejected because there is no chief in the Iroquois Confederacy analogous to the US President. Option C can be rejected because the Iroquois Confederacy did not involve representation based upon a tribe's population. Option D can be rejected because there was no judicial branch in the Iroquois Confederacy analogous to that of the US government.

73. B: Hammurabi's Code, a code by for ancient Babylonian society written by Hammurabi (king of Babylonia), is among the earliest written codes of law and helped establish a precedent for codifying law. Rather than restructuring Babylonian society, the Code described and codified many existing practices; this eliminates option A. Option C can be eliminated because Hammurabi's Code did not establish the same penalties for all law-breakers; rather, according to the Code, punishment depended in part upon the offender's social status, as well as that of the victim. Option D can be rejected because the Code included many punishments involving death or mutilation.

74. A: Democracy of ancient Athens was direct rather than representative: citizens voted directly on issues rather than elected representatives doing it for them. Answer B can be rejected because the right to vote did not depend on a person's wealth or a on a person's family's wealth. However, voters did need to have Athenian parentage, and only free men could vote; women and slaves could not. Rather, Athens took pains to ensure that poor people could participate politically. Option C can be rejected because there were no political campaigns in Athens as they are understood today; many political positions were chosen by lot, i.e., men did not campaign for them. Finally, some actions could result in losing the right to vote; this eliminates option D.

75. C: Cases involving diplomats and ambassadors automatically fall under the jurisdiction of the Supreme Court.

76. B: Discretionary spending is dedicated to transportation, education, national resources, the environment, and international affairs. State and local governments use this money to help finance programs. Mandatory spending covers entitlements such as Medicare, Social Security, Federal Retirement, and Medicaid.

77. C: Primary sources are sources that were created at the time of the event in question. For examples, recordings of Martin Luther King's speeches, newspaper accounts of King's activities at the time of those activities, and King's written documents are all primary resources regarding Martin Luther King's work. Secondary sources, such as a history book that contains a subchapter on the work of MLK, are secondhand and are almost always created after the fact. This eliminates choice A. Secondary sources do not need to be text-only, nor visual only, as the example above illustrates; this eliminates both options B and D.

78. A: The passage is a firsthand account of witnessing, via television, the first moon landing, and is best suited for teaching students what that experience was like. Although the source does briefly describe the surface of the moon, this description is not the main idea of the passage and is too brief to be well-suited for a unit on this topic. This eliminates option B. Option C can be eliminated because the author of the passage makes clear that he or she was very young at the time of the landing, and the author explicitly states that he or she is not clear how it was possible to show the moon landing live on earth. Finally, option D can be rejected because although the author does describe a change the author's family's own television, the passage makes no general claims about changes in television use.

79. D: A claim is biased when it is not objective but instead tilted in favor of a perspective. In this case, the author's use of "our" in the sentence, "That just showed again how our technology, American technology, had become much more advanced than Russian technology," shows that the author is American and identifies with American achievements. This in and of itself does not demonstrate that the author's claim is biased but illustrates that the author reasonably has a motivation for making a claim biased in favor of American technology. Further, because the author was young when he or she had the thought about technology, and because there is no indication that the author had been to Russia or studied technology, there is no foundation to show that the author used any objective criteria when rendering his or her opinion. There seems to be no similar motivation for the claims in the other options to be biased.

80. A: Case studies typically involve gathering qualitative data, such as data acquired through personal observations of the subjects of the case study, or by interviewing the subjects of the case study. Less common in case studies is the gathering of quantitative data. Because a typical case study does not gather quantitative data, it also does not involve statistical analysis. This eliminates options B and C. Finally, option D can be eliminated because common research methods in case studies, such as interviews, do not involve an absence of contact between a researcher and the subjects of the study.

81. A: Critical writing involves evaluation, not merely the reporting of information. Because option A asks students to make a claim and defend it, it requires students to practice their critical writing skills. Options B and D can be rejected because they do not involve this sort of evaluation or judgment, but merely the reporting of information. Option C is not the best choice because creative work does not necessarily involve making arguments or giving reasons, i.e., does not necessarily involve explicit argumentation in the way that critical writing does.

82. A: The most reasonable inference based on the data given by the map is that the areas with no shading (which represent areas of low water use) are less inhabited than areas with shading. Note that the areas with no shading also have no listed cities; cities on the map are surrounded by shaded areas. Because the map does not give any information regarding how much water is required per capita, option D can be rejected. The map gives no indication regarding residents' prowess at conservation efforts (positive or negative). This eliminates option C. Additionally, there is no indication from the map that any land is more desert-like. In fact, some of the lightly-shaded area is adjacent to the ocean. Therefore, option B can be rejected.

83. A: The apparent distance between Greenland and Norway will be greatest on a Mercator map. The Mercator map is a type of cylindrical projection map in which lines of latitude and longitude are transferred onto a cylindrical shape, which is then cut vertically and laid flat. For this reason, distances around the poles will appear increasingly great. The Mercator map is excellent for navigation because a straight line drawn on it represents a single compass reading. In a conic projection map, on the other hand, a hemisphere of the globe is transposed onto a cone, which is then cut vertically (that is, from rim to tip) and laid flat. The apparent distances on a conic projection will be smallest at the 45th parallel. A contour map uses lines to illustrate the features of a geographic area. For example, the lines on an elevation contour map connect areas that have the same altitude. An equal-area projection map represents landmasses in their actual sizes. To make this possible, the shapes of the landmasses are manipulated slightly, and the map is interrupted (divided into more than one part).

84. C: Roman numeral III indicates the Colorado River. The Colorado River begins in Colorado and journeys through Arizona, Utah, and Nevada along the border of California, and into Mexico. The Colorado River is a major river; it is responsible for carving out the Grand Canyon, and is important for agricultural use and other uses. Roman numeral I indicates the Snake River. Roman numeral II indicates the Sacramento River. Roman numeral IV indicates the Rio Grande River. Each of these rivers is a major river in the United States, but all are separate bodies of water from the Colorado River.

85. A: The distance between Buenos Aires and Tokyo is approximately 18,060 km. The process of converting a scaled distance to a real distance is fairly simple. In this case, multiply the number of centimeters by the number of kilometers represented by each of these centimeters. The calculation can be expressed as (35 cm) (516 km/1 cm). Because centimeters are in the numerator of the first term and the denominator of the second term, they cancel out, leaving kilometers as the unit.

86. C: After precipitation, the heat of the sun causes evaporation, a process by which water molecules change from a liquid to a gas, ultimately returning to the atmosphere. The other options describe processes that pertain to properties of water, but not to water's return to the atmosphere. Percolation is the process by which water moves down through soil. Cohesion (specifically, structural cohesion) is the property of matter by which the molecules in a single substance stay together. Condensation is the process by which matter changes from a gas to a liquid; after evaporation, molecules of water form rain droplets through condensation.

87. B: The Southern Hemisphere of the Earth experiences winter when the Northern Hemisphere experiences summer because of the angle of the Earth. The Earth rotates on its tilted axis as it orbits the sun. At different positions in its orbit, the axis is tilted toward or away from the sun to varying degrees. The sun shines more brightly and directly on one hemisphere than the other, causing the difference in seasons. When a hemisphere is tilted toward the sun, that hemisphere experiences its summer season. Options A, C and D all fail to give a good explanation for the difference. It is neither the changing distance from the sun nor the changing speed of the Earth's orbit that causes the difference in seasons, though these attributes do fluctuate slightly. Also, the shape of the earth does not cause the difference in seasons.

88. A: Rivers promoted the development of the ancient river valley civilizations of the world, including in the Middle East, India, and China. Rivers not only supply water for drinking and crop irrigation, but also provide fertile soil, vegetation for shade cover, food, building materials, and animal life. They additionally allow water travel to other locations. Although some peoples have settled and lived in deserts, they are among the most inhospitable climates. Forests also provide plenty of flora and fauna and exist in areas receiving enough rainfall, but rivers have been historically superior in attracting human societies. Mountains near living areas provide protective barriers; however, though some peoples live there, as in deserts, living in the mountains is difficult due to high altitudes, harsh climates, poor soil for planting, and rough terrain.

89. A: In desert environments, where little rain falls, some animal species have adapted by estivating during the day, thus allowing the animals to escape the desert's searing daytime heat. The other answers can be eliminated because the associated climates are not nearly as hot, removing the impetus for an animal to avoid the daytime heat. The climate of a tundra, for example, is much cooler, and in that environment it would make much less sense for an animal to avoid daytime heat. This eliminates answer C. Options B and D can be rejected because the climates of the temperate forests and grasslands are not as hot as that of deserts, providing less reason for animals to adapt by estivating.

90. A: World population growth has significantly affected global deforestation, as forests have been cleared for agricultural use, livestock, and timber harvesting. World population growth has not lead to increased biodiversity. Global biodiversity has actually shrunk in response to humanity's exponential population growth; this eliminates option B. Similarly, ocean dead zones—regions featuring low concentrations of oxygen—have grown in the last decades rather than shrunk; this eliminates option C. Finally, although there have been mass extinction events throughout earth history (such as those involving dinosaurs), they are not linked to world population growth; this eliminates option D.

91. B: The highest habitable region in Middle and South America is known as the *puna*, or *páramos*. This region ranges in altitude between 12,000 and 15,000 feet and lies primarily in the Andes Mountains. Only sheep and other rugged livestock can be herded at this height, so there is very little economic activity. *Tierra fria* lies just below the *puna*, between 6,000 and 12,000 feet in elevation. It is possible to cultivate wheat at this height. The *tierra helada* is an uninhabitable region over 15,000 feet high, just above the *puna*. This region is always covered in snow and ice. The *templada*, also known as the *tierra templada*, is a moderate region between 2,500 and 6,000 feet high. Coffee, corn, and tobacco can all be grown in this region.

92. A: Despite its size, China has only 11 percent of usable land for farming, or just a little over 1 million square kilometers. For this reason, China consistently remains one of the largest importers of food in the world.

93. D: The Ka'ba is an ancient structure Muslims consider holy; it was purportedly built by Abraham. The Ka'ba's location in Mecca is the central reason for Mecca's importance to Muslims. Although Muhammad was born in Mecca, that fact is not the primary reason for Mecca's importance in Islam; the location of the Ka'ba is more important. This eliminates option A. Option C can be rejected because Muhammad fled from Mecca to Medina in 622 AD, not the other way around. Option B can be rejected because Muslims believe the Second Coming will occur in Damascus, not Mecca.

94. B: According to Buddhism, life is full of suffering. However, by following the Noble Eightfold Path, the path of moral living, it is possible to end suffering. Samsara, the cycle of birth, death, and rebirth, is an important concept in Buddhism, but it is not the Noble Eightfold Path; therefore option A can be rejected. Regarding option C, there are Precepts in Buddhism that offer a guide to Buddhist ethical behavior; these are related to the Noble Eightfold Path, but they are not the same; this eliminates option C. Finally, while self is an illusion according to Buddhist doctrine, this view is not the substance of the Noble Eightfold Path. This eliminates option D.

95. A: Stephen's routine is considered by geographers to be cyclic movement. This type of movement happens regularly, does not involve traveling over a great distance, and does not require a change of residence. Because Stephen returns home every evening, he cannot be said to be changing residence. A migratory movement is a permanent change of residence, especially from one country or region to another. A cross-boundary movement is any change in location that involves crossing a national border. A periodic movement is similar to a cyclic movement, except it takes place over a longer time. Going to college for a semester is an example of periodic movement.

96. A: Built in the nineteenth century, the Suez Canal provided the shortest water route between Europe and Asia by connecting the Mediterranean Sea with the Gulf of Suez and the Red Sea (not the Black Sea; this eliminates option B). This had the effect of allowing Europeans greater access to Asia, which led to further trade between Europe and Asia, as well as European colonization of Asia. Option C can be rejected because the Suez Canal has been the specific focal point of violence in the

Middle East, for example between Egypt and Israel. Option D can be rejected because the main significance of the Suez Canal is that of a trade route rather than a military route.

97. A: North Africa is not one of the world's four major population agglomerations. These are eastern North America, South Asia, East Asia, and Europe. The largest of these is East Asia, which encompasses Korea, Japan, and the major cities of China. The second-largest population agglomeration is South Asia, which includes India and Pakistan. Most of the population in this area is near the coasts. The European agglomeration is spread across the largest piece of land, while the much smaller agglomeration in eastern North America is primarily focused on the string of cities from Boston to Washington, DC.

98. A: Hamilton has the greater population density. Population density is a measure of the number of people living in a particular area. It is usually calculated in units of citizens per square mile or square kilometer. The respective population densities of these two towns, then, can be calculated by dividing the number of citizens by the number of area units. So, the population density of Hamilton is 400 / 12 = 33 citizens per square mile, and the population of Burrsville is 300 / 10 = 30 citizens per square mile.

99. B: Diversity is not one of the demographic variables. Demographers, or those who study population, rely on fertility, mortality, and migration to determine the number of people in a region. The general equation is *Total Population = Original Population + Births – Deaths + Immigration – Emigration*. The natural increase, on the other hand, is calculated only with the number of births and deaths. The diversity of a population may be relevant to subsequent research performed by the demographer, but it is not considered one of the essential three demographic variables.

100. D: One result of NAFTA, the North American Free Trade Agreement, has been that Mexico has sought to enter into other trade agreements. After the implementation of NAFTA in 1993, trade barriers among Canada, the United States, and Mexico were removed. The goal was to encourage economic activity within all three countries. There continues to be a lot of controversy over NAFTA's success, and it was eventually replaced with USMCA, United States-Mexico-Canada Agreement.

101. B: Economists understand the true cost of an action as not only its monetary cost but the cost of other opportunities missed as a result of pursuing that action. For example, if a person chooses to go to school rather than working, the cost of the action involves not only tuition and other associated fees and expenses, but the money one would have earned working, as well as the time one could have spent pursuing other activities. The concept of opportunity cost is not described by options (A), (C), or (D), each of which is concerned only with monetary costs. Each of these answers can be rejected on that basis.

102. D: Keynes was an influential advocate of government intervention in a domestic economy for the purpose of stimulating economic growth. Keynes believed that appropriate government action could help end a recession more quickly; such measures might involve deficit spending. Because of this, and because Keynes is not associated with the view that deficit spending leads to inflation, option A can be eliminated. Additionally, Keynes is not closely associated with advocating government action to break up monopolies; this eliminates option B. Finally, option C can be eliminated because it describes Say's Law, which is in fact the opposite of Keynes's law: demand creates its own supply.

103. A: Eli Whitney's invention of the cotton gin, a mechanism for quickly separating cotton seeds from cotton fiber, helped elevate cotton as a basis of the Southern economy. Option B can be rejected because, rather than leading to smaller plantations, the invention led to larger cotton plantations. Choice C can be rejected because the United States did not need to import cotton; rather, particularly after the invention of the cotton gin, the United States became a leading exporter of cotton. Finally, option D can be rejected because with larger plantations came an increased need for slaves: the cotton gin had the effect of increasing dependence on slave labor rather than decreasing it.

104. C: The graph shows a shift in demand, with a corresponding increase in the price of SuperCell Batteries. The shift is illustrated by the two demand curves, with Demand 2 curve illustrating an increase in price. Because the price has increased, not decreased, this eliminates option A. The equilibrium point is the point at which the quantity demanded equals the quantity supplied. The graph shows two equilibrium points, the first where Demand 1 meets the supply curve, and the second where Demand 2 meets the supply curve. Because equilibrium has shifted, option B can be eliminated. Regarding option D, a double coincidence of wants occurs when two people each have a good or service the other wants, giving rise to the possibility of trade (without money). The graph does not illustrate anything regarding a double coincidence of wants, so option D can be rejected on that basis.

105. C: A key to the question is the relation between supply and demand. The use of graphics in presentation software can be used effectively to show supply and demand curves, which effectively show the relation between supply and demand. Neither options A and B explain the relation between supply and demand; option A merely involves listing such terms, and B merely involves understanding the terms in isolation, but not the relation between them. Option D can be rejected because it concerns only demand, not supply and demand.

106. B: Only option B requires a student to take knowledge of supply and demand and consider how each component interacts with the other, i.e., to analyze the concepts. To interpret a supply curve is to consider how supply affects demand and vice versa in a particular case. Option A requires the giving of information of supply and demand, but not the application of it; option A can therefore be eliminated. Options C and D, though related perhaps to supply and demand, do not explicitly call for the application of particular knowledge of supply and demand. Options C and D, then, can both be rejected.

107. A: When a company has a monopoly, it is the sole supplier of a good or service and therefore exercises great control over the price of that good or service. In an oligopoly, a small number of companies supply a given good or service (these companies might also act to control prices of that good or service). Because a monopoly differs from an oligopoly in this fundamental way, options B and D can each be rejected, as those answers describe an oligopoly as a kind of monopoly. Also, a monopoly might involve only one plant, but it could just as easily involve more than one; the distinguishing feature of a monopoly is its control over supply, not the number of plants or factories it uses in production. This eliminates option C.

108. D: In the short run, a perfectly competitive firm should shut down if total costs exceed total revenue and if the total variable costs exceed total revenue. If total revenue exceeds total variable costs, the firm should continue production. The difference between total revenue and total fixed costs is not part of this determination.

109. B: Unemployment leads to lost productivity because people who would be productive if employed (thus contributing to economic growth) are not economically productive when they do not have work. Option A can be rejected because high unemployment is not typically thought to be a central cause of inflation; rather, high levels of unemployment might instead contribute to deflation (an overall decrease in prices). Option C can be rejected because unemployment would tend to have the effect of decreasing aggregate demand rather than increasing it, simply because fewer people would have money with which to make purchases. Option D can be rejected because unemployment is less likely to increase aggregate supply than to reduce it (fewer people working means fewer people producing goods and services).

110. C: Economists are interested in unemployment caused by changes in the business cycle. That is what cyclical unemployment measures. There will always be some measure of structural and frictional unemployment, and those are not typically considered when assessing the unemployment picture in a nation.

111. C: Inflation is an overall increase in prices. Inflation commonly occurs when there is a large amount of printed currency circulating in an economy at a time when there are few available goods relative to that amount. Options A and B can be eliminated because each describe conditions under which deflation occurs (an overall falling of prices, the opposite of inflation). Option D can be rejected because when there is a relatively low amount of currency circulating within an economy together with a relatively low number of available goods, prices are not apt to rise.

112. D: In the long-run Phillips Curve, unemployment stays at the natural rate of unemployment (NRU). As a result, while price levels change increase and decrease, movement along the long-run Phillips Curve is only up or down.

113. A: Corporations offer limited liability protection, unlike sole proprietorships. For example, the person running a corporation is not personally liable for the debts of a corporation to the extent that a person running a sole proprietorship is for the debts of the proprietorship. In a sole proprietorship, the sole proprietor has unlimited liability for the debts of the business. Note that such debts include ordinary operating expenses, tax liability, liability from lawsuits, etc. Option B can be eliminated because corporations run afoul of the "double tax" problem when the person running a corporation (who pays himself from the company earnings) pays tax on the company's earnings twice, first via the taxes assessed against the corporation itself and second via his or her own personal income tax. Corporations are more expensive to form than sole proprietorships, but this is a disadvantage; this eliminates option C. Option D can be eliminated because corporations are more difficult to dissolve than sole proprietorships.

114. A: The Sherman Antitrust Act outlawed "every contract, combination ... or conspiracy in restraint of trade or commerce among the several States, or with foreign nations." Option C describes trade within states; because the Sherman Antitrust Act does not address such trade, option C can be rejected. Options B and D each describe a use of the Sherman Antitrust Act; i.e., the Act was instrumental in breaking up both the Standard Oil trust and the AT&T monopoly. However, neither of these particular uses are as influential as the general outlawing of acts restraining trade between states; rather, it was the general prohibition which made these particular applications (and others) possible. This eliminates options B and D.

115. D: None of the options listed are true. Excess reserves will increase by \$80,000, as the bank must keep 20% of the deposit, or \$20,000, leaving \$80,000. The money multiplier is one divided by the reserve ratio, or 5 $\left(1 \div \frac{1}{5} = 5\right)$. This means the money supply could increase a total of \$500,000 ($\$100,000 + (5 \times \$80,000) = \$500,000$).

116. D: The Federal Reserve has the power to buy and sell government bonds to or from banks, thereby raising or reducing interest rates. When banks buy government bonds, they have less money available to loan, and interest rates are higher; when banks sell bonds, they have more money available to loan, and interest rates are lower. Option A does accurately describe a tool of the Federal Reserve, but not a tool the Federal Reserve uses frequently; the same is true of option C, and therefore both options A and C can be rejected. Option B can be eliminated because the Federal Reserve does not buy or sell stock options to change interest rates.

117. C: If a country's currency increases in value, foreigners will have to give up more of their own currency to get the original country's currency in order to buy the original country's goods and services. This will cause a drop in exports. At the same time, it will be less expensive for people in the original country to exchange their currency for foreign currencies, causing the price of imported goods to drop and the total value of imports to rise.

118. D: When demand for a foreign currency drops, the value of that currency drops. This makes it cheaper to buy goods from that foreign country.

119. A: Converting nominal GDP to real GDP requires some measure of the change in prices of goods and services within a nation over time. One could use the Consumer Price Index—the value of a fixed "market basket" of goods and services on a yearly basis—to determine the rate of inflation and then adjust nominal GDP to real GDP.

120. A: Although some of Wundt's questions may have overlapped with those of philosophers, Wundt tried to test his views by collecting data. In doing so, he helped establish psychology as an empirical science. A central component of Wundt's methodology was asking subjects to report their internal perceptions, or to introspect. However, modern psychology does not make use of this method; this eliminates option D. Wundt's method also eliminates option B; Wundt's views depended on reports of internal perception, rather than relying on publicly-observable behavior. Wundt wrote voluminously on many topics but often changed his mind; this eliminates option C.

121. B: The graphic best illustrates the concept of stratification. In sociology, stratification is the hierarchical structure or organization of human society. Because the chart indicates a hierarchical division of traditional Indian society (dividing society's members according to caste, with Brahmins occupying the most elevated position), the chart illustrates stratification. Assimilation is the process of an individual or group adopting the customs of another group; the graphic does not illustrate this process and option A can therefore be rejected. Diffusion occurs when a culture borrows ideas from another; socialization is the process by which an individual learns a culture. As the graphic illustrates neither of these processes, both options C and D can be rejected.

122. A: According to John Locke's version of social contract theory, when human beings are in the state of nature (prior to entering a social contract), each person has a right to punish another for breaking the moral law. Because it is not always feasible for someone to punish anyone else for such an offense, people form the social contract in part to delegate the right to punish to certain individuals. Option B can be rejected because Locke thought natural law provided a basis for moral behavior, and natural law was independent of a social contract. Option C can be rejected because Locke believed that humans had natural rights inherently, i.e., that these rights were not conferred on them by a social contract. Finally, option D can be rejected because it describes Thomas Hobbes's view of the state of nature; Locke held a less pessimistic view.

123. B: Reification is the act of treating an abstraction as a real, concrete thing. For example, the concept of society might be useful, but it is not an actual, concrete thing separate from the components (such as people and infrastructure) that make up society. Options A, C, and D can all be rejected because none accurately capture the concept of reification. Social scientists might indeed be concerned with relative appropriateness of qualitative data and quantitative data, but using one over the other is not reification. Social scientists might use heuristic devices, but this is not simply reification (not all cases of reification are cases of using heuristic devices). Reification is not mistaking subjectivity for objectivity.

124. C: Learning such an association is classical conditioning. Generally, classical conditioning is the process of learning an association between two stimuli, one of which is neutral (in this instance, the sound of the can opener) and one to which an organism responds automatically (in this instance, food). Habituation occurs when an organism becomes desensitized to a repeated stimulus; this eliminates option B. Operant conditioning differs from classical conditioning in that, in the former, an organism changes its behavior in response to reinforcement (that is, an organism can change the outcome of an event by changing its behavior). This eliminates option A. Conformity is the process by which an organism changes its behavior to match others' behavior. This eliminates option D.

125. B: Anthropology is the study of the origin and development of humankind and is much less concerned than psychology with individual human behavior (psychology is the study of the human mind and behavior). Psychology and anthropology both involve natural sciences, for example information about how the brain works; option A can rejected on that basis. Anthropologists commonly use qualitative methods as well as quantitative methods; this eliminates option C. Finally, option D can be rejected because anthropology involves more than a study of physical human evolution; it also includes subjects such as culture and language, for example.

126. D: Early civilizations flourished alongside rivers such as the Nile in Egypt, the Euphrates in Mesopotamia, and the Yellow River in China. Besides providing the ancient settlers with a water source, these rivers also provided the land with the rich and fertile silt that the rivers deposited during their regular flooding cycles, making large scale agriculture possible for the ancient peoples.

127. D: In Charles Darwin's theory of evolution, natural selection is the mechanism by which species evolve. Darwin posited that there is a variation of characteristics in individual organisms within a species. Some characteristics better equip individual organisms to survive and reproduce. When these organisms reproduce, their offspring are likely to inherit those advantageous characteristics. Over time, the species itself may evolve based on the widespread inheritance of such characteristics with survival value. Therefore, natural selection is concerned with the evolution of species as a whole, rather than adaptation of individual organisms. This eliminates choice B. While environmental pressures can play a role in natural selection, natural selection does not describe the diversity of such pressures. This eliminates choice A. Answer C can be rejected because Darwin did not believe characteristics acquired during an organism's lifetime were inherited.

128. B: Cognitive psychologists seek to explain individual differences between humans by studying how people think and come to acquire knowledge. This is the best answer for the question. Regarding option A, although a cognitive psychologist might study how society influences a person's beliefs, this description is too narrow to constitute the best answer. In other words, a cognitive psychologist doesn't just look at the influence of society on an individual's thought processes, but studies those thought processes independent of such influence. This eliminates option A. Option C can be eliminated because it describes the approach of the clinical psychologist (not the cognitive psychologist), and option D can be rejected because it describes a biological approach (not that of the cognitive psychologist).

129. B: The President may veto legislation passed by Congress. The executive branch has this "check" on the legislative branch.

130. D: Einstein's special theory of relativity, which he proposed in 1905, postulated the relativity of simultaneity (also the relativity of motion), i.e., that there is no absolute simultaneity. What counts as simultaneous depends on one's frame of reference. Some of Einstein's later work, but not his 1905 special theory of relativity, pertained to constructing a unified field theory; this eliminates option A. Option B can rejected because Einstein's famous work on gravity occurred later, not in his special theory of relativity. Option C can be rejected because Einstein did not believe that the speed of light is relative; rather, it is constant no matter one's frame of reference.